Attacking Faulty Reasoning

T. Edward Damer
Emory and Henry College

Wadsworth Publishing Company
Belmont, California
A Division of Wadsworth, Inc.

For Nancy Jean

Philosophy Editor: Kenneth King
Production Editor: Carolyn Tanner
Designer: Janet Wood
Copy Editor: Susan Weisberg

Printed in the United States of America

3   4   5   6   7   8   9   10——84   83   82

Library of Congress Cataloging in Publication Data

Damer, T. Edward.
　　Attacking faulty reasoning.

　　Includes index.
　　1. Fallacies (Logic)　2. Reasoning.　I. Title.
BC175.D35　　　　　165　　　　　79-13883
ISBN 0-534-00750-3

Contents

"appeal to personal circumstances"
, p. 121, 2nd ed.

Preface

One of the most disturbing aspects of my teaching experience has been that the students in my philosophy classes who come to understand and recognize fallacious thinking are only rarely able to use this knowledge effectively. They fail to understand that simply charging someone with an error in reasoning usually serves no constructive purpose and, indeed, often creates ill feeling. Hence, the impetus for writing this book was to suggest some ways of confronting errors in reasoning that might be constructive, that is, might turn fallacious thinking into sound thinking.

Some of the distinctive features of the book are these: (1) Only the most common errors are treated; (2) each section begins with a clear, concise definition of the fallacy in question; (3) every effort is made to use believable examples about relevant issues; (4) positive strategies are suggested for confronting every faulty pattern of thinking, with special attention given to the so-called absurd example method; (5) some of the traditional fallacies are renamed to be more informative; (6) some traditional definitions are reformed in order to avoid confusion with other fallacies; (7) exercises are provided at the end of each chapter as a self-testing aid; (8) a second set of exercises, which is cumulative, accompanies each chapter in order to assist the reader in regularly reviewing previous material.

The book is intended for use as a text in any course that gives special attention to critical thinking and sound reasoning. It is especially recommended as an auxiliary text for an introductory course in philosophy or an introductory course in logic. It is designed in such a way that only a small amount of in-class time need be spent in discussing the fallacies. On the basis of experimental use of the material in this book, it is my judgment that most students can come to understand and recognize instances of these fallacies simply by reading and studying the text. The instructor would probably need to do little more than prepare periodic tests similar to those at the end of each chapter.

The treatment of each fallacy follows the same pattern. Following a concise definition, there is a brief commentary on why that particular pattern of reasoning is fallacious. Where appropriate, the fallacy is distinguished from other fallacious and nonfallacious patterns with which it might be confused. There is often a very fine line between a fallacious and a nonfallacious form of reasoning, and careful distinctions need to be made.

For each of the fallacies studied, several examples illustrate the error in question. However, such illustration creates a particular pedagogical difficulty. Clear-cut examples do not frequently appear in real-life situations, and clear-cut "textbook" examples are rarely believable. In real-life situations, not only is it often the case that several different fallacies are committed in a single argument, but also the error in question is often subtly blended with quite correct and persuasive forms of reasoning. This is particularly the case when the argument extends over several paragraphs or throughout a lengthy discussion. The typical textbook examples created to meet this problem are usually not convincing, as readers don't believe that anybody would actually commit such obvious errors. I have made every effort to select or create both clear-cut and believable illustrations of each fallacy. Following each set of examples, there is an "attacking the fallacy" section, which offers some specific suggestions for attacking or exposing the particular fallacy in question.

The two types of exercises at the end of each section provide the opportunity to identify fallacies from an ever-expanding variety of forms. Readers thus will progressively approximate typical real-life situations. The answers to all the exercises are provided at the end of the text.

The last chapter of the book gives attention to a number of syllogistic and other formal fallacies and is written in a highly compressed form. Yet it is comprehensive enough that it should assist the careful reader in recognizing and responding to a few of the most commonly committed fallacies of deductive inference. However, as this material is more technical and probably more difficult than other parts of the book, an instructor may prefer not to assign it. A reader who desires a general acquaintance with the most common formal as well as informal errors in reasoning may appreciate the inclusion of this material.

There are several people who have been especially helpful in the preparation of this book. My colleague in philosophy at Emory & Henry College, Richard A. O'Neil, read the entire manuscript and made many helpful suggestions, which have been incorporated into the text. Lawrence L. Habermehl, of American International College, read an earlier draft of the definitions of the fallacies. At his suggestion, a number of the originally proposed fallacies were either eliminated or combined with others. My wife, Nancy Jean Bradford, deserves special credit for her assistance in construction of many of the examples used; for her incisive criticism, which led to the refinement of many of the book's sections; and for her consistent encouragement of the project. To my students in philosophy I express my gratitude for their suggestions, which led to some of the examples and some of the refinements in the definitions and commentaries. I also wish to express appreciation to Emory & Henry College, from which I received two summer grants that provided some financial support for the project.

Introduction

It has been my experience that few people are really interested in a careful study of logic, because, as Charles Peirce suggested, "everybody conceives himself to be proficient enough in the art of reasoning already."[1] It is interesting to note, however, that the "proficient" individual rarely grants to any other person a similar proficiency. Few arguments other than one's own are regarded as genuinely sound, and it is sincerely believed that what the rest of the world needs is "to study a little logic."

The study of logic is primarily a process of learning to think correctly and to express oneself as clearly as possible. One of the purposes of this book is to assist in that process by giving attention to some of the most common errors in our ordinary ways of thinking. However, because I believe that little constructive purpose is served by simply learning to identify errors, I hope that the facility developed in recognizing mistakes in reasoning may lead to constructive principles of sound reasoning. Hence, my purpose in focusing attention upon errors is ultimately that of helping others to construct arguments that "make sense."

A second purpose is to suggest some concrete ways of challenging faulty reasoning when it is directly encountered. I am convinced that in most cases it is possible to confront one's verbal opponent with his or her faulty reasoning without creating any ill feeling. Moreover, it can be done in a way that will move a debate beyond the question of who has committed the worst fallacy to the question of what can be reasonably inferred. Therefore, the strategies that are suggested for each fallacy are designed to get reasoning back on the right track, that is, to turn faulty

[1]Charles Sanders Peirce, "The Fixation of Belief," in *Collected Papers of Charles Sanders Peirce*, ed. Charles Hartshorne and Paul Weiss (Cambridge, Mass.: The Belknap Press of Harvard University Press, 1934), V, 223.

reasoning into sound reasoning. They are designed to assist faulty arguers in doing what they allegedly wish to do—to argue in convincing and nondeceptive ways toward the objective of establishing the truth of a claim or belief.

These strategies may also help to alleviate another problem often created by faulty reasoning—the feeling of helplessness that one often experiences when one is the target of fallacious reasoning, a feeling that results from simply not knowing any effective way to deal with the error in question. I hope that the suggestions accompanying the treatment of each fallacy will assist one in gaining control of the situation by exposing the error and redirecting the line of reasoning toward more constructive ends.

Kinds of Arguments

The kind of correct or sound reasoning that I am concerned about is that found in arguments. By *argument*, of course, I am not referring to a bitter controversy or heated disagreement. I have in mind the attempt that is made to proceed from premises, that is, statements of evidential support, to a particular conclusion by means of orderly and reasonable inference. In most cases, the errors to which I call attention are those committed in the process of constructing or responding to such arguments.

Arguments may be divided into two categories: deductive and inductive. A *deductive* argument is one whose form is such that the conclusion follows with logical necessity or certainty from the premises. In other words, if the premises are true, the conclusion must be true.[2] For example:

All Senators in the U.S. Senate are 35 years old or older.

Howard Baker is a U.S. Senator from Tennessee.

Therefore, Howard Baker is 35 years old or older.

The conclusion of this or any deductive argument simply spells out what is already implicitly contained in the premises.

An *inductive* argument is one in which the premises provide *some* evidence for the truth of the conclusion. However, the conclusion of an inductive argument does not follow with logical necessity or certainty from the premises, even if all the premises are true. For example:

Howard Baker is the highest ranking Republican in the Senate.

He is very personable and articulate.

He is a political moderate on most issues.

He easily won reelection to his Senate seat.

He is in great demand on the speaking circuit.

[2]Another way of describing the relationship between the premises and conclusion of a valid deductive argument would be to say that it is impossible for such an argument to have true premises and a false conclusion. One could not accept the premises and deny the conclusion without contradicting oneself.

He is often mentioned by prominent Republicans as a possible presidential candidate.

Therefore, Senator Howard Baker will be chosen by the Republicans as their next presidential nominee.

The conclusion of this or any inductive argument is at best only probable, not certain. The reason is that the conclusion makes a claim that goes beyond the evidence provided in the premises, a claim that is not implicitly contained in the premises. Therefore, in an inductive argument, in contrast to a deductive argument, the truth or acceptance of the premises does not force or guarantee the truth or acceptance of the conclusion.

Sound Arguments

An argument is sound if it meets all the following criteria: First, the premises of the argument must be true. Second, the conclusion must follow from the premises. If the argument is *deductive*, it must be patterned after a valid logical form; that is, the form of the argument must be such that the truth or acceptance of its premises forces or guarantees the truth or acceptance of its conclusion. If the argument is *inductive*, the premises must strongly confirm the truth of the conclusion. Third, the content of the argument must be free of problems such as linguistic confusions, irrelevancies, circularities, inconsistencies, or any unwarranted assumptions.

This book will not deal with the complex problems related to the first criterion, except to say that if an argument has a premise that you suspect of being dubious or untrue, you should attack it directly at that point. Either call upon your verbal opponent to give evidence of the truth of the questionable premise or provide your own evidence against its truth. In any case, you should reject any argument whose premises remain questionable; for any conclusion based upon a doubtful premise will be equally doubtful.

The concern of this book is with the second and third criteria of a sound argument. Arguments that have an invalid deductive form are generally regarded as formally fallacious. Those arguments whose premises do not strongly confirm their conclusions and those arguments with other problems in content are usually regarded as informally fallacious.

What Is a Fallacy?

In ordinary language, the term *fallacy* is used broadly to refer not only to an error in logic but also to a mistaken or false belief. This book restricts the term to the context of reasoning. In most cases, a fallacy is a mistake in reasoning, and a fallacious argument is one that contains such an error. The term is also used to refer to such things as linguistic confusions or diversionary devices, which lend themselves to error in reasoning or to the obstruction of clear thinking processes.

Fallacious arguments are usually quite deceptive, and their erroneous quality is sometimes not easy to detect. Hence, such arguments may be psychologically quite persuasive. The deceptiveness of an argument, of course, need not be intentional; but I make no attempt to distinguish between intentional and unintentional deception. To make such a distinction, in most cases, is extremely difficult. Moreover, the question of whether one intentionally or unintentionally uses faulty reasoning is, in my judgment, a question not of logic but of ethics.

Because an argument that contains an error is most likely to lead to a false conclusion, a rational person should be dissuaded from accepting the conclusion of such an argument. Even if a fallacious argument should, by some means, lead one to a true conclusion, there are usually no good reasons provided by the argument for believing it to be true.

Why Study Fallacious Reasoning?

There are at least three reasons one might benefit by studying the fallacies in this book. First, being able to discriminate between fallacious and nonfallacious reasoning is a necessary condition of sound reasoning. Focusing attention upon mistakes in reasoning should assist one in avoiding them. Such study, then, should contribute to one's own intellectual integrity. Second, familiarity with some of the most common errors in reasoning is a defense against being misled or victimized by others. Third, because one's own fallacious reasoning and that of others often lead to false beliefs and thus to foolish, if not harmful, consequences, an ability to avoid faulty reasoning may have serious moral implications. For this reason, it could even be argued that one is morally obligated to become acquainted with common patterns of fallacious reasoning.

Deliberate Use of Fallacious Reasoning

As I indicated above, there is no attempt in this book to make a distinction between intentional and unintentional uses of fallacious reasoning. A fallacy is a fallacy, regardless of whether it is intentionally committed. There are, however, several good reasons for avoiding any *deliberate* use of fallacies. First, in most cases, the deliberate use of fallacious arguments has the same character as lying. The liar tries to get another person to regard as true that which the liar knows to be false. Similarly, one who deliberately uses fallacious reasoning tries to get another person to accept as a sound argument for a claim that which the arguer knows to be quite unsound. Therefore, deliberate fallacious reasoning is justified only if lying can be justified.

Second, intentional use of fallacious reasoning often has the effect of obscuring the truth, and so it would seem to me that any person who is genuinely interested in achieving a reliable understanding of the world and his or her own place in it would want to avoid any kind of fallacious reasoning. Therefore, a deliberate use of fallacious reasoning comes into direct conflict with a serious interest in arriving at the truth.

Third, false beliefs, to which fallacious arguments sometimes lead, often result in actions that can and do cause considerable harm. Therefore, if one deliberately engages in erroneous argument, one could be blameworthy for any harmful consequences that may ensue.

Finally, because fallacious reasoning is often easily detected by one's listeners, a person who is interested in maintaining an image as a clear thinker will probably want to avoid being caught in an act of defective thinking. One factor that motivates me to engage in nonfallacious reasoning is my own interest in avoiding such intellectual embarrassment.

Who Commits the Fallacy?

It is sometimes assumed that the only person who can commit a fallacy is the one who constructs arguments. However, those to whom arguments are presented also bear responsibility for avoiding errors in reasoning. People who reason fallaciously by accepting a fallacious argument as a sound one are just as guilty of committing a fallacy as those who use a fallacious argument in an attempt to convince others of a particular point of view. In most cases, the fallacies studied in this book are formulated primarily in terms of their being committed in the process of constructing arguments; yet those to whom arguments are addressed generally must also exercise care in avoiding faulty reasoning by refusing to accept the conclusions of faulty arguments.[3]

Naming the Fallacies

This book will give attention to those distinguishable errors in reasoning that occur regularly in human discourse. Most of these patterns of faulty reasoning have been exhibited so frequently that they have even been assigned specific names. To be able to identify particular patterns of fallacious reasoning is important; for to say of an argument simply that it is "illogical" or that "something seems wrong with it" is not helpful in eliminating the problem. It is analogous to the situation of one who does not feel well, goes to a doctor, and is told: "You're sick!" If a medical problem or a fallacious argument is to be effectively treated, it is first necessary to diagnose the problem. In the case of a fallacious argument, a diagnosis entails specifying just what makes the argument fallacious.

Various systems of classifying or grouping faulty patterns of reasoning have been used by textbook writers on logic. My particular organization of the fallacies into ten different categories probably represents more of a departure from traditional schemes than do most systems. I hope that the larger number of

[3]Only a few of the fallacies studied are formulated primarily in terms of their being committed by the listener: namely, the fallacy of illicit contrast, false ambiguity, and misuse of vague expressions.

categories will help to focus attention on some of the common features of the fallacies in each class and thus make them easier to detect. For example, there are a number of begging-the-question fallacies, all of which commit the same basic error; but each one does so in a distinguishable way.

Each of the fallacies in the book is assigned to a particular category, but each is given a very precise description or definition. In most cases, this definition is restricted to one or two sentences. Although the definition could conceivably be memorized, it is more important that readers understand and translate it into their own language. The concise definition, then, is hopefully more of an aid to understanding than an encouragement to memory.

No special effort is made to preserve the traditional names for the fallacies studied. For example, traditional Latin names are maintained in only three cases — the *post hoc* fallacy, the *ad hominem* fallacy, and the *tu quoque* fallacy. The reason for retaining these Latinisms is the relative familiarity of these terms in ordinary discourse. My intention to assign names that will give some indication of the actual character of the error has led me to abandon several traditional names. For example, I have given the name misuse of a generalization to what has been traditionally referred to as the fallacy of accident; and I have replaced the term fallacy of ignorance with the term fallacy of negative proof. In all cases, I have not hesitated to create new names or to alter old names when the traditional ones do not help to identify the fallacious patterns in question.

There is a definite advantage in being able to detect a fallacious pattern of reasoning by name. If a pattern of faulty reasoning is so common that even a name has been assigned to it, there is considerably less uncertainty that it is fallacious. For example, during the early days of the Watergate investigation, a conservative southern senator publicly criticized Senator Edward Kennedy for raising questions about former President Nixon's possible wrongdoing. The senator claimed that Kennedy had no right to criticize others in view of his own personal problems.[4] When, at a social gathering, I alluded to that kind of thinking as committing the fallacy of *tu quoque,* my listener remarked with some element of relief, "You mean there is a name for that kind of thinking? I thought there was something wrong with it. I just wasn't sure what it was." It seemed intellectually reassuring to her to discover that that particular kind of reasoning had been specifically identified by logicians as fallacious, even to the point of having been assigned a name. If a fallacy has a name, we are assisted in recognizing it more readily and confidently when we encounter it in an argument. To know well the enemies of sound reasoning is the first step in overcoming them.

Rules of the Game

Argument with other people, like other sports, must be played in accordance with certain ground rules. However, in this case, the rules I have in mind are not the rules of correct reasoning. To detect violations of or to encourage conformity to those rules is part of the game itself. The ground rules I am referring to here are

[4]I presume that he was alluding to the so-called Chappaquiddick incident.

those that relate to the psychological context of the game, that is, the rules of good sportsmanship. If you wish to maintain healthy, friendly relationships with your verbal opponents, and if you hope ultimately to win your point with the least amount of embarrassment and bitterness, I suggest that attention be given to the following guidelines:

First, don't be a fallacy monger. Some people, with a little bit of knowledge of fallacious reasoning, often develop a kind of methodological obsession with identifying fallacies in the utterances of others. They sniff suspiciously at every argument and point of debate. Such pouncing upon others creates more alienation than clarification. Several students have reported to me that while taking my course in logic they experienced considerably more difficulty in relating to their friends, parents, and other professors. My thinking is that these difficulties stem from a kind of fallacy mongering, wherein one attempts to point out, in a pedantic fashion, all the fallacies in even the most casual comments of one's friends and acquaintances.

Second, confront verbal opponents with their fallacious reasoning only when you are convinced that a false conclusion has been reached as a result of a particular error in reasoning or in order to explain why you find the conclusion of the argument unacceptable. To point our errors that have no significant bearing upon the basic thrust of the argument may only delay the progress of the debate and divert attention away from the point at issue.[5]

Third, when you yourself are caught committing a fallacy, admit the mistake and make the appropriate adjustments in your thinking. Don't try to deny the charge or explain it away by making excuses or by claiming you were misunderstood. Don't be a sore loser.

Finally, avoid the word *fallacy* altogether, if possible. There are subtle ways of informing verbal opponents that they have committed an error in reasoning without having to shout: "Aha! That's a fallacy!" Because names assigned to fallacies often vary from list to list and because people are often "turned off" by technical jargon, the wisest course of action would be to find ways of focusing attention upon the pattern of faulty reasoning itself. Be imaginative. Find ways, such as those discussed below, of challenging the reasoning processes of others without alienating them or causing them unnecessary embarrassment. After all, our purpose is to assist people in thinking more clearly, not to catch them in a fallacy.

Absurd Example Method

One of the most imaginative and effective ways of dealing with instances of fallacious reasoning might be called the absurd example method. This method is a way of demonstrating faulty patterns of reasoning without appealing to technical

---

[5]In general, it is a good policy to expose a fallacy regardless of whether it leads to a false conclusion in a particular context, because failure to challenge such a pattern of reasoning could encourage its continued use in other contexts. However, in most situations this policy must be cautiously weighed against the possibility of sidetracking discussion of the more substantive issues at stake.

jargon or rules. It is particularly effective on people unfamiliar with or unimpressed by the special names and distinctions used by professional logicians.

This method can be used on both formal and informal fallacies. The following example shows how it might be effectively used on formal fallacies. Suppose a verbal opponent claimed that, as all communists are atheists (all A are B), and all humanists are atheists (all C are B), one must conclude that all humanists are communists (all C are A). Such an argument has true premises but a false conclusion, which means, by definition, that the argument cannot be a valid one. In order to demonstrate the faulty character of this kind of reasoning, you might point out that the middle term of this standard syllogistic argument is undistributed, which is a sufficient condition for its invalidity.[6] However, you would probably be more persuasive, especially to the logically untutored, if you compared the original argument to another argument with the same form but with an obviously false or absurd conclusion. For example, you might say that, as all fathers are parents (all A are B), and all mothers are parents (all C are B), one must conclude that all mothers are fathers (all C are A). The premises are true, the argument has the same form as the original, but the conclusion is obviously false and even absurd. Thus, it should be clear to your opponent that his or her argument is also faulty, since it follows the same pattern of reasoning found in the absurd example.

The same method can be used on most informal fallacies. Suppose that an antiabortionist argued in the following manner: "Because the fetus at birth is generally regarded as a human being, and because it would be arbitrary to insist that at some particular point in the term of pregnancy the alleged nonhuman fetus suddenly becomes a human being, it could be concluded that the fetus at conception is no less a human being than it is at delivery." This kind of faulty reasoning exhibits what has been characterized as the difficulty of the slippery slope; yet it is a very persuasive form of arguing. In order to demonstrate the faulty character of this kind of reasoning, you could point out that the antiabortionist's argument commits the "fallacy of the continuum"; that is, it assumes that supposed contraries or extremes, as long as they are connected by intermediary small differences, are really much the same.

A better approach, however, might be to compare the form of the antiabortionist's argument with another argument of the same form but with an obviously false conclusion. For example, because an atmospheric temperature of 100°F is generally regarded as hot, and because it would appear to be arbitrary to insist that, at some particular point during a period in which the temperature rises from 40°F to 100°F, the alleged nonhot temperature suddenly becomes hot, one could conclude that 40°F was really no less hot than 100°F. Such a conclusion is obviously false. It should therefore be clear that the antiabortionist's conclusion is unwarranted, as the pattern of reasoning is similar to that in the absurd example. I am not saying that the antiabortionist's conclusion is false; I am simply saying that this particular argument should not lead one to the antiabortionist's conclusion; because it follows a pattern of reasoning that has been shown to be faulty.

[6]See Chapter X.

It is often difficult to produce an absurd example on the spot, so it might be wise to keep a standard absurd example in mind for most of the fallacies. It is important to point out, however, that the absurd example method of confronting others with their mistakes in reasoning is not easy to master; it requires considerable practice, imagination, and a very thorough understanding of the most common patterns of faulty reasoning.

Conclusion

One of the main purposes of an education is to develop the ability to discover and to defend conceptually reliable ideas about ourselves and our world. A careful study of this book should be of help in accomplishing that aim. Because it is likely to expose some of the careless and defective ways that you have examined or defended your own ideas in the past, you may come to believe that not only the rest of the world but you also may need "to study a little logic." Although this may be a somewhat unsettling experience, be comforted by the fact that it is one of the most important steps toward making sense.

I
Fallacies of Linguistic Confusion

The fallacies discussed in this chapter result from some misuse of or confusion in the meaning of the words, phrases, or sentences used in arguments. Words, regardless of how refined they may be, are always a potential source of misunderstanding. A change in context can cause a subtle change in the meaning of a word or even a whole sentence. If careful attention is not given to this phenomenon of language, one can be seriously deterred from making appropriate inferences. Therefore, anyone who is interested in sound thinking must be aware of the imprecision of our language as one of the first steps toward helping to clarify and stabilize meanings. We should also be able to identify particular patterns of reasoning that are based upon the misuse of, or confusion in, our linguistic utterances. The fallacies listed below are the most common errors of this kind.

Equivocation

Definition: This fallacy consists in directing an opponent toward an unwarranted conclusion by making a word or phrase, employed in two different senses in an argument, appear to have the same meaning throughout.

The soundness of any argument requires that the words or phrases employed retain the same meanings throughout the argument unless a shift in meaning is understood or specified. To equivocate is to make it appear that two words have the same meaning, when in fact they do not. Deception of this kind is particularly difficult to detect in long arguments in which the transition in meaning can be well concealed. Even though a word or phrase functions in one part of an argument in quite a different sense than it does in another, it can be used in such a way that support is given to the claim at issue simply because the words have the same appearance or sound. It is quite possible, of course, that an arguer may be unaware that the words in his or her argument have shifted in meaning; however, the fallaciousness exists whether or not it is intentional or recognized.

In syllogistic reasoning, equivocation takes place if one of the terms of the syllogism shifts in meaning. Because a standard categorical syllogism may have three and only three terms, each of which appears exactly twice in the argument, a subtle change in the meaning of a term renders the argument formally fallacious. Equivocation in such a case is often referred to as the fallacy of four terms.[1]

It might be helpful to point out that a pun, by definition, depends upon the possibility of a word's having multiple meanings. What makes a pun clever or humorous is that the listener will momentarily fail to recognize that the term in question has shifted in meaning. In no way am I suggesting that one should avoid the happy practice of punning. I would insist, however, that if you are seriously attempting to justify a substantive claim, you should guard against allowing the words in an argument to shift their meaning.

Finally, remember that the listener bears as much responsibility for avoiding fallacious reasoning as the person who has constructed the argument. For example, if you fail to recognize a shift in the meaning of a term within the context of another person's argument, you will also be guilty of committing the fallacy of equivocation, for, through your own carelessness, you are allowing a fallacious argument to be a convincing one.

Example: "I don't see any reason why we should listen to the superintendent of schools on this textbook issue. We need to hear from someone who has some authority in the field of education. Our superintendent doesn't even have enough authority to keep the students *or* the teachers in line. Nobody respects her orders." The first use of the word *authority* refers to a person who is competent in a particular discipline or field of inquiry. The second use of the word *authority* refers to the ability to maintain order or to command respect for or compliance with one's wishes. The issue, of course, is whether the superintendent has sufficient training and competence in the field of educational theory to be considered an authority in that field. If she is such an authority, her judgment deserves to be heard. However, the shift in meaning of the word *authority* could lead one to think that she is not an authority in the first sense.

Example: "You say that all of our actions are determined, but I know some people who never seem to know what they are going to do or how they are going to behave. They simply never give thought to their actions ahead of time. Hence, I would say that, at least for those people, it would not be accurate to say that their actions are determined." The first use of the word *determined* refers to the view that actions can be wholly accounted for in terms of antecedent conditions. The second use of the word *determined* refers to actions that are deliberate or carried

[1]Syllogistic fallacies are treated in Chapter X.

out with firm convictions. Because of this illegitimate shift in meaning, you could be misled into thinking that the respondent had provided evidence against the claim that the actions of all people can be accounted for in terms of antecedent conditions.

Example: "My college adviser suggested to me that I should take logic because logic, he said, teaches one how to argue. But I think that people argue too much as it is. Therefore, I do not intend to take any course in logic, and I am of the opinion that perhaps logic shouldn't be taught at all. It will only contribute to increasing the tension that already exists in the world." The first use of the word *argue* refers to the process of carefully supporting claims with evidence and sound reasoning. The second use of the word refers to a bitter controversy or to a kind of disagreeable haranguing between individuals. The shift in the meaning of the word *argue* might lead you to think that you ought to avoid taking a course in logic for reasons that are irrelevant to that conclusion.

Attacking the Fallacy: If you have reason to believe that you are being confronted with an argument involving equivocation, there are at least two ways of dealing with its fallacious character. One way would be to identify the problematic word or phrase and point out to your verbal opponent the two different ways the word functions in the argument in question. If there is some dispute about whether the arguer has equivocated, you may ask for precise definitions of the suspected words or phrases. If the definitions are different, then the charge will be proved. Another way to demonstrate the fallacious character of reasoning that involves equivocation is to use the absurd example method. For example:

Only man is rational.

No woman is a man.

Therefore, no woman is rational.

The equivocation on the word *man* leads to a conclusion that is obviously absurd.

Semantical Ambiguity

Definition: This fallacy consists in presenting a claim or argument that uses a word or phrase that can easily be interpreted in two or more distinctly different ways without making clear which meaning is intended.

Almost every common word in our language has more than one meaning; hence, there is obviously nothing fallacious about using a word with more than one meaning. The fallacy of semantical ambiguity exists when the context of the argument does not make clear which of the several meanings of a word is intended. If the context does not help clarify the intended meaning of the term in question, it is quite possible that a listener might interpret the word in another way and thus arrive at a false conclusion.

Example: Suppose a friend said to you: "Yesterday we moved into a new house." It is probably not clear from the context whether the "new" house is a different house or a recently constructed one. Hence, it would be inappropriate for you to draw any conclusion about the kind of structure in which your friend now resides.

Example: Newspaper headlines are often semantically ambiguous. If you read only the following headline, it would be difficult to draw any justifiable conclusion: ELIZABETH TAYLOR LOSES APPEAL. It would be impossible to know, without reading the article, whether Ms. Taylor had ranked low in a recent poll ranking the world's most beautiful women, whether she is now no longer a box-office attraction, or whether she had just lost a case that she had appealed to a higher court. The newspaper editor has therefore committed the fallacy of semantical ambiguity, and the reader should draw no conclusion without reading the article.

Example: Consider this familiar scene with two people driving in city traffic:

Laura: You'll have to tell me how to get there.
Eleanor: Okay. Turn right here. [Laura turns right.] Hey, I didn't mean for you to turn *right*! Couldn't you see that I was pointing left?

In this case, of course, Eleanor meant for Laura to turn *immediately,* but as Laura did not happen to see Eleanor's pointing, her verbal directions were surely ambiguous.

An even more familiar ambiguity encountered in the context of driving is as follows:

Laura: Do I turn left here?
Eleanor: Right!

No matter whether Laura subsequently turns right or left, Eleanor's directions must again be pronounced ambiguous, for it is unclear whether Eleanor is simply confirming Laura's assumption or suggesting another direction.

Attacking the Fallacy: As in the case of the fallacy of equivocation, you should identify the confused or ambiguous word and, if possible, ask the speaker for the intended meaning. If it is not possible to make such a request, use your own knowledge of the larger perspective of the speaker as a clue to the possible intended meaning. If neither of the above is possible, you might hypothesize about the intended meaning and draw a very tentative conclusion based upon that speculation. If the conclusion is consciously tentative, it can be more easily changed with additional information or clarification.

Syntactical Ambiguity

Definition: This fallacy consists in making a claim that can be legitimately interpreted in two or more distinctly different ways because of its grammatical construction.

Syntactical ambiguity is distinguishable from semantical ambiguity by virtue of the fact that it can be "cured" by a grammatical reconstruction of the sentence. In contrast, semantical ambiguity is remedied by a clarification of the meaning of the particular ambiguous word or phrase. To learn to avoid syntactical ambiguity, become aware of some of the particular forms of this fallacy. Some of the most typical grammatical errors that render a sentence ambiguous are: unclear pronoun reference ("Claude never argues with his father when he is drunk"); elliptical construction[2] ("John likes logic better than his wife"); unclear modifier ("I have to take my make-up test in an hour"); careless use of *only* ("The tennis courts will be available to members only from Monday to Saturday"); and careless use of *all* ("All of the fish Doug caught weigh at least fifteen pounds"). Such ambiguous constructions are often referred to by grammarians as *amphiboles*.

Example: Suppose you were to read a brochure about a school of carpentry that said: "Come to our school and learn how to build a house in six weeks." It would be unclear whether you are going to be taught in a six-week course how to build a house or whether you are going to learn at the school of carpentry ways of constructing a house within a period of six weeks. A reconstruction of the sentence could clarify the intended meaning.

Example: "The minister delighted everyone with his brief sermon." It is not clear whether the people were entertained by the sermon or simply happy that he confined his remarks to a brief time span. Again, the intended meaning could be clarified by a syntactical rearrangement of the sentence.

Example: Two colleagues who live near each other are preparing, after a late afternoon meeting, to leave the campus for their homes. Their homes are in walking distance of the campus, but because it is raining, one says to the other: "How about a ride home?" It is quite possible that the one to whom the question is addressed might think that he is being offered a ride home in the automobile of the asker. On the other hand, it may be the case that the asker is herself seeking some means of transportation home. If the one who was asked the question answers "Okay," it is not clear whether he is agreeing to give the asker a ride home or accepting the asker's offer of a ride. If neither had an automobile parked on campus and if the ambiguity were not cleared up before they walked to the parking lot, it is quite possible that the two colleagues might find themselves standing in the rain looking stupidly at each other in the middle of an empty parking lot. At least that was the way I experienced it a few years ago. The false conclusions and embarrassment to which we were led by the grammatical structure of my question could have been avoided if I had been more careful in formulating it.

Attacking the Fallacy: Ask the speaker for a translation of the sentence into other words *or* for a grammatical reconstruction of it until you are satisfied that

---

[2]The omission of one or more words that are supposedly understood but that must be supplied in order to make a sentence grammatically complete.

you understand the intended meaning of the sentence. Other suggestions for dealing with this fallacy are similar to those regarding semantical ambiguity.

False Ambiguity

Definition: This fallacy consists in a listener's drawing an improper conclusion by carelessly interpreting a word or phrase with two or more different meanings in a manner not justified by the context.

The responsibility for this fallacy is borne entirely by the listener. If you *deliberately* interpret a word, phrase, or sentence in a way not justified by the context, probably you are simply attempting to be a punster, in which case no fallacy is committed. The fallacy *is* committed, however, when you interpret a word, phrase, or sentence in an unjustified way because of careless attention to the context. When the careless respondent is called upon to justify such a peculiar interpretation, he or she typically places the blame upon the original speaker; but the original speaker has not committed the fallacy of ambiguity if the context makes clear the proper interpretation of the language.

Example: Consider the road sign that indicates there are "Free Picnic Tables Ahead." It would surely be a case of false ambiguity if one were to infer that picnic tables are being given away. Highway travelers could be reasonably expected to understand that many people carry picnic lunches with them as they travel. Hence they should more properly infer from the sign that there are picnic tables ahead that may be used by the public without obligation to purchase local food or drink.

Example: Suppose you received from the publishers of a magazine to which you had subscribed a letter that included the following statement: "The magazine to which you have subscribed is being discontinued, but a substitute magazine of comparable worth will be sent to you until your expiration date." You would commit the fallacy of false ambiguity if you assumed that you would receive the substitute magazine for your entire lifetime. The context of the letter clearly indicates that *expiration date* refers to the previously contracted length of the original subscription.

Example: If you were told that Professor Provost teaches crime courses at the University of Missouri, it would be fallacious to assume that she teaches people how to become criminals. In a case like this, you would be expected to utilize your general understanding of what goes on at state-supported universities. You could be reasonably assured that people at such schools are not taught to be criminals. The larger context, then, would suggest that crime courses are probably courses taught in the Department of Sociology that deal with the phenomenon of crime in our society, the causes of crime, and possibly the treatment of the criminal.

Attacking the Fallacy: People who are inclined to interpret words and sentences in ways not justified by their context should be directly confronted with their erroneous reasoning. The most direct way of exposing this kind of thinking is to point out just what it is about the context that makes the interpretation in question unjustified. If it is your own statement that has been misinterpreted, don't be intimidated if your opponent attempts to place the blame upon you. Shift the responsibility to him or her as quickly as possible by showing how the context of your statement did not allow for such an interpretation. If you need an absurd example to illustrate your point, you might use the following one:

> **Buck:** Why did you take off all your clothes?
> **Lila:** Because when I asked you if you would like to see my new dress, you said that you would like nothing better.

Obviously, Lila has carelessly taken Buck's earlier remark in a manner that is justified neither by its context nor by ordinary linguistic usage.

Fallacy of Accent

Definition: This fallacy consists in directing an opponent toward an unwarranted conclusion by placing improper or unusual emphasis upon a word, phrase, or particular aspect of an issue or claim. The fallacy is sometimes committed by lifting portions of a quotation out of context in such a way as to convey a meaning not intended by the person quoted.

This fallacy is sometimes quite difficult to detect, as it can result from the slightest change in the speaker's voice inflection. Many sentences can take on quite different meanings depending on which word is being stressed or given an unusual emphasis. Such stress is sometimes given by means of a sarcastic or mocking intonation. If such accenting causes a listener to come to an unwarranted conclusion, even though the words themselves might not express an untrue statement, the speaker is guilty of misleading.

Example: If a father were speaking of the problems of raising his three children and said of his oldest daughter: *"She* won't listen to me" (stressing *she*), you might conclude that the other two children *do* listen to him. If it is not the case that the other two children do respond positively to him, the father might be justifiably accused of directing his hearers to a false conclusion, even though the words that he uses express a true proposition.

Example: A student says: "I often see Professor O'Neil, but never with his *wife."* The particular stress on the word *wife* in this sentence would probably suggest that Professor O'Neil spends a great amount of time with someone other than his wife *or* that he never takes his wife anyplace. The sentence itself, without stress on any particular word, may express a true proposition—namely, that the student has not seen Professor O'Neil with his wife. However, because of the accent on the word *wife,* a listener may be led to infer one of the other two interpretations of the statement.

Example: Newspaper headlines and titles of magazine articles often commit the fallacy of accent. Again, the actual words of the headline or title may be the vehicle for a true statement, yet the statement may be misleading in that it suggests some additional claim because of an unusual stress. Such headlines or titles often lead to understandings that are put into proper perspective only by the articles to which they are attached. This is commonly the case with movie magazines and "scandal sheets." For example, several months after the death of Aristotle Onassis, one such magazine used the following title for one of its articles: TEDDY CONFIRMS RUMOR: JACKIE WILL BECOME A KENNEDY AGAIN. The title could lead readers to the conclusion that Senator Kennedy would be divorcing his wife, Joan, and marrying Jackie Onassis. To enforce this interpretation, the front cover and the article each carried a picture of Ted and Jackie in a tender pose. However, the article simply suggested that the Kennedy clan still considered Jackie to be a part of their larger family. Suppose the following headline were printed in your local newspaper: BILLY GRAHAM FAVORS HOMOSEXUALS. The headline might lead one to infer something about Reverend Graham's sexual interests, whereas the article might be simply an item from an interview in which Graham said that he saw no reason why repentant homosexuals should not be ordained into the ministry.

Example: One of the most frequently committed forms of the fallacy of accent is lifting a phrase or sentence out of its context. Emerson's statement that "a foolish consistency is the hobgoblin of little minds" is commonly used to denigrate the attempts of others to avoid contradiction. However, the larger context of Emerson's essay suggests the proper interpretation of his statement:

> *A foolish consistency is the hobgoblin of little minds, adored by little statesmen and philosophers and divines. With consistency a great soul has simply nothing to do. He may as well concern himself with his shadow on the wall. Speak what you think now in hard words and tomorrow speak what tomorrow thinks in hard words again, though it contradict every thing you said today.* [3]

It is clear that Emerson is cautioning against such a reverence for past thoughts that one hesitates to speak one's mind in the present simply because one's present thoughts may differ from those held in the past. In other words, he is challenging the tendency to be reticent about changing one's views. Emerson clearly does not mean to encourage logical contradiction.

Attacking the Fallacy: In most cases, you can confront the fallacy of accent like the other fallacies of ambiguity already treated. Take particular care to read or ask for the larger context of any statement you suspect of being accented. You might preclude the possibility of being misled by questionable headlines or

[3]Ralph Waldo Emerson, "Self-Reliance," in *Documents in the History of American Philosophy*, ed. with commentary, Morton White (New York: Oxford University Press, 1972), p. 175.

titles by determining, if possible, to read the articles to which they are attached. At least you can be very cautious about drawing an inference based on a headline or title alone. In general, it is always wise to follow the rule of "when uncertain, ask." Don't be embarrassed to ask about something you don't understand. It is better to run the risk of appearing naive or uninformed than to come to a false conclusion.

Illicit Contrast

Definition: This fallacy consists in directly inferring from a claim some related but unstated contrasting claim by placing improper or unusual emphasis upon one of the words or phrases in the statement.

This fallacy is very closely related to the fallacy of accent, but in this case it is clearly the listener, rather than the speaker, who does the accenting. It is also similar to the fallacy of false ambiguity insofar as it involves drawing a conclusion that is not justified by the context. In the case of illicit contrast, one is claiming that the speaker accented some particular part of a claim that led to the inference drawn, even though there is no evidence that any such emphasis was introduced by the speaker. Indeed, it is the listener who has introduced the misleading emphasis.

Example: If a young woman, after some unhappy love affair, claimed that men are insensitive brutes, it would be fallacious to infer from her statement that she was implicitly contrasting males to females, saying that females are *not* insensitive people. The young woman was not trying to characterize the differences between men and women; she was probably just responding emotionally to her own hurt feelings. Moreover, even if she were making the claim that all men are insensitive, nothing should be inferred about her thinking regarding the sensitivity of women.

Example: If a Catholic cardinal were dealing with a problem in which a young priest had been discovered to be relating sexually to a married woman, he might caution all the priests in his diocese that: "It is improper for priests to relate sexually to married women." It would be fallacious, since it would be unjustified by the context, to assume that the cardinal is suggesting that it is *not* improper for priests to relate sexually to *un*married women, or that it is not improper for *non*-priests to relate to married women.

Example: The following conversation between my two daughters and me took place recently in my home:

Father: Isn't that Diana's dress you have on, Cynthia?
Cynthia: It's mine now. Diana gave it to me. It's too little for her.
Father: Well, it looks very nice on you.
Diana: Then you don't think it looked nice on *me*?

In this short domestic exchange, Diana committed the fallacy of illicit contrast, for she falsely accused me of accenting the word *you* when I said, "It looks nice on you." The case was, however, that I did not stress the word *you*; I was simply describing how the dress looked on Cynthia. I was making no implicit comment on how it looked or might have looked on someone else.

Attacking the Fallacy: Because one who commits this fallacy is falsely accusing the speaker of accenting some particular part of a claim that led to the questionable inference, you should insist that the burden of proof is upon the accuser to demonstrate that the context or voice inflection of the speaker encouraged such an interpretation. Such a proof, however, is not easy to produce, for the speaker has a peculiar advantage. The speaker can almost always charge the accuser with committing this fallacy simply by pointing out that the contrasting claim was not *specifically* uttered, even though the context or emphasis might be such that the contrasting claim was clearly intended. In this case, of course, the fallacy of illicit contrast would not be committed. The concern here, however, is how to attack the fallacy when it *is* committed. No person should be required to accept responsibility for any claim not made. If you think that you have been falsely accused of making a claim that you have not made, you might simply address (or express willingness to address) the claim in question, making it quite clear that your original statement had in no way implied that claim.

Argument by Innuendo

Definition: This fallacy consists in directing one's listeners to a particular, usually derogatory, conclusion, by a skillful choice of words or the careful arrangement of sentences, which implicitly *suggest* but do not *assert* that conclusion. The force of the fallacy lies in the impression created that some veiled claim is true, although no relevant evidence is presented to support such a view.

This method of arguing is commonly used to attack a person, group, or idea when there is little or no evidence to justify a straightforward claim or accusation. The power of suggestion is used in this way to compensate for the lack of relevant evidence. Because no actual claim is made, it could be said that a person using the argument by innuendo is not guilty of outright lying or of making an unjustified claim. Indeed, such a speaker would probably deny that any outright claim had been made and would refuse to accept responsibility for any inference that might be drawn from his or her utterance.

Example: Sometimes the addition of a single word or phrase in an utterance can lead to a false or unjustified conclusion, even though the words together do not express anything that is not true. Suppose that a dean of students at a college is asked by an employer if a prospective employee had ever been in any kind of disciplinary difficulty while attending college. The dean might look at the records and say, "No"; or she might say, "No, we were never able to convict him of any violations of college rules." The latter response, unfortunately, would probably have a negative effect on the prospective employee's chances for employment, even though it might express a true proposition. Suppose that the prospective employee were still a student at the college in question and the dean said in response to the same question: "No, not yet!" The addition of the last two words transforms a straightforward negative answer into one filled with innuendo. Moreover, the further conclusion that the employer might draw from such a response is one for which the dean would probably not wish to accept responsibility.

Example: Suppose that you heard the following statement uttered by one of the candidates in a hard-fought gubernatorial race: "If you knew that one of the candidates in this race were receiving money from illegal sources, would that affect your voting decision? Look into the matter and see where the campaign funds of my opponent are coming from. The facts might surprise you." The speaker has allegedly made no serious claim against his opponent that requires any kind of defense; but the power of suggestion has done its work.

Example: The power of innuendo usually depends upon the tone of the speaker:

> **Ginger:** Are Allison and Eddie still going steady?
> **Luci:** Well, according to Eddie, they are.

The straightforward claim is that Eddie believes that he and Allison are going steady. The tone of the response could suggest that Eddie is unaware that Allison thinks differently about their relationship or even that Allison is dating other men — a fact unknown to Eddie.

Example: One of the most effective means of engaging in innuendo is using words that sound like other words with negative connotations and counting on the listener's making the desired association. Of course, one must know one's audience well to make effective use of this form of innuendo. A textbook published a few years ago contains a very clever example of this form:

> While addressing a group of farmers during his first campaign for the Senate, a certain Senator is reported to have said of the man he subsequently defeated: "Are you aware that my opponent is known all over Washington as a shameless extrovert? Not only that, but this man is reliably reported to have practiced nepotism with his sister-in-law, and he has a sister who was once a thespian in wicked New York. He matriculated with coeds at the University, and it is an established fact that before his marriage, he habitually practiced celibacy."[4]

Attacking the Fallacy: In spite of the fact that the speaker usually will not wish to take responsibility for the unspoken claim, you should perhaps spell out the conclusion to which you have been led and ask the speaker to justify it. In no case should you accept an implicit claim without being satisfied on evidential grounds, for an implicit assertion requires the same justification as does an explicit one. If the speaker is not inclined to defend the claim in question, suggest that he or

[4]Peter T. Manicus and Arthur N. Kruger, *Essentials of Logic* (New York: American Book Company, 1968), pp. 354–355.

she specifically both deny the implicit claim and take definite steps to counter-balance the effect that it has had. Finally, be especially careful that you do not read innuendoes into utterances when they are not there.

Misuse of Vague Expressions

Definition: This fallacy consists in drawing an unjustified conclusion as a result of assigning a very *precise* meaning to another's word, phrase, or statement that is quite *imprecise* in its meaning or range of applicability. The fallacy may also be committed by one who attempts to establish a position by means of a vague expression.

A person is not guilty of committing this fallacy simply because he or she employs vague expressions. The fallacy occurs when vague expressions are mis-used, that is, when a very particular conclusion is inferred from an obviously vague expression. Vagueness, then, becomes a problem when its presence might encour-age a false or unjustified conclusion and when there is something of substance at stake in the discourse. Vague expressions may also pose another peculiar problem in argumentation. For example, if a vague term is used in support of some particu-lar claim, that support is at best dubious. Moreover, such a statement, by virtue of its vagueness, is almost impossible to refute.

Example: At a recent faculty meeting, the president of our small college told us that our student enrollment figure was moving us toward a financially dangerous low point and that perhaps we should show a little more concern for some of our weaker students, some of whom were dropping out of school because of failing grades. In response to the president's remarks, one faculty member indig-nantly exclaimed that he would quit before he would let the president force him to give a passing grade to a student who did not deserve it. The faculty member, in this case, gave a particular interpretation to the president's vague request to "show a little more concern for some of our weaker students." Of course, if previous experience gave the faculty member reason to believe that "show a little more concern" was a euphemism for "don't fail any students," then his interpretation would have been justified. In this instance, however, such was not the case.

Example: A recent Supreme Court ruling regarding pornography in-cluded the view that what is "pornographic" should be determined in accordance with "community standards." However, a prosecutor who tried to establish a case against a distributor of pornographic materials on the grounds that he or she had acted in violation of "community standards" would have to assign a very precise meaning to that very vague criterion—a precision to which it does not lend itself. By assigning such meaning, one might reasonably be charged with misusing a vague expression.

Example: During a textbook controversy in southwest Virginia, some people claimed that the use of the *Responding* series of textbooks constituted a violation of a state law that requires public schools to engage in "moral education." The critics claimed that to use literature with profane or obscene language was to teach school children immoral ways of behaving. Such literature, it was said, taught students to be *im*moral. Here is a case where a very particular interpretation is given to the very vague phrase *moral education.*

Attacking the Fallacy: Avoid drawing any particular conclusion from an obviously vague statement. If the range of applicability is definitely indeterminate, ask for a more precise application of the expression. In most cases, vague expressions can be attacked like ambiguous expressions; that is, you can insist upon further clarification or stipulation of meaning. To follow such a procedure is particularly important if the discourse is substantive and if it is desirable to continue the debate. If nothing significant is at stake, you can, of course, simply ignore the imprecision. If you yourself wish to avoid being misunderstood, avoid using imprecise words as much as possible. Find new words to replace those that have become hopelessly vague, or at least specify the meaning of any words that may have become too vague in ordinary usage to convey your intended meaning precisely.

Distinction Without a Difference

Definition: This fallacy consists in attempting to defend an action or point of view as different from some other one, with which it is allegedly confused, by means of a very careful distinction of language. In reality, however, the action or position defended is no different in substance from the one from which it is linguistically distinguished.

Probably the most common occasions of this fallacy are when an arguer wishes to diminish the possible embarrassment he or she feels in holding what is probably an untenable position or when one's behavior is questionable. One is free, of course, to stipulate the meaning of any term he or she uses, but if the new meaning functions in the same way that the original meaning functions, no difference is made by the attempted distinction. Moreover, as the fallacy is usually committed in response to some form of accusation, the alleged distinction, because it really constitutes no difference in meaning, does not blunt the force of the accusation.

Example: Suppose the question is whether a particular person is a good driver. It is generally agreed that the ordinary "good driver" obeys the rules of the roads, keeps his or her mind upon the task of driving, and is courteous to other drivers. Suppose that the individual in question is easily distracted by events taking place along the road and frequently turns and talks to other people in the car, thus failing to see and respond appropriately to important road signs. The response to the accusation that he is not a very good driver might be, "I'm not really a bad driver; I just don't pay much attention to the road." The accused person has made a distinction that exhibits no real difference. Hence, the force of the accusation against the driver has not actually been blunted.

Example: Suppose your roommate plays her stereo louder than you can comfortably tolerate. When you complain that the stereo is too loud, she may respond by saying, "It's not too loud; it's just that you and I like to listen to music at very different dynamic levels." From your point of view, your roommate has not answered the charge; she has only repeated it in different words. To say that you enjoy the music more if it is played at a lower volume says nothing substantially different from saying that you think it is "too loud" when it is played at a higher volume.

Example: "I'm not saying anything against women's lib; I just happen to sincerely believe that the male should be the head of the household." This is an example of a very familiar attempt to hide one's opposition to the antisexist movement. At best it represents a confusion concerning the issue of sexism. In any case, the distinction drawn is an empty one.

Attacking the Fallacy: Because many people are unaware that their attempted distinctions are not true differences, the first step that you might take is to try to point out to them the futility of their efforts. If your verbal opponent takes issue with your assessment, which is likely, you might ask for an explanation of just how the alleged distinction differs in meaning. If you are unconvinced by this explanation, you may be inclined to offer a lesson in semantics. But as that would probably not be fully appreciated, why not settle for the absurd example method? Consider the following example: "I wasn't copying; I was just looking at her paper to jog my memory." Such an example should clearly illustrate how very different words can function in very similar ways.

Exercises

Identify the type of linguistic confusion in each of the following:

1. **A:** In the college handbook concerning cafeteria regulations, it says: "Appropriate dress is expected at all times."
   B: That's terrible. Why should I have to wear a coat and tie just to eat in the cafeteria?
2. **A:** Statistics show that few people die after 95.
   B: That's ridiculous; no one lives forever!
3. Jimmy Connors defeated Ken Rosewall before a crowd so partisan that it forgot its traditional sportsmanship to applaud his errors.
4. Last term I took logic and introduction to philosophy. I hope I have more exciting courses this term.
5. I don't know anything about Elliott, except that he's a liberal, so I didn't

vote for him. I didn't want to add another voice to the ranks of the critics of the military in the Congress.

6. Nan is a very poor artist.

7. Gambling should be legalized because it is something we can't avoid. It is an integral part of human experience; people gamble every time they get in their cars or decide to get married.

8. A: I sure feel good today.

B: I didn't realize that you had not been feeling well.

9. A new play in town was evaluated by the local newspaper's drama critic as being "a great success, considering the lack of facilities and the poor quality of actors with whom the director had to work." The play was then publicized as "A great success. . . ."

10. What is right should be required by law. To vote is a right in the United States. Therefore, there should be a law requiring people to go to the polls and vote.

11. A headline in a country newspaper reads: TWO DOCTORS FOR 50,000 PATIENTS. The article to which it is attached explains that there are only two veterinarians for the estimated 50,000 animals in the county.

12. I didn't lie to you; I merely stretched the truth a bit.

13. Senator Phillips reported that the changes in the bill introduced by the Democrats have improved it considerably.

14. A: Is Valerie helping with the charity show this year?

B: Well, she comes to our meetings!

15. Student to faculty adviser: "If I were smart, I would major in math."

16. A: I just don't see how I can do what you want me to do, doctor.

B: What do you mean?

A: How can you take one of those pills twice a day? That's impossible!

17. An impartial arbitration committee should not take sides when settling a dispute. But the so-called impartial committee that was supposed to arbitrate the issue between the students and the administration decided in favor of the administration and suspended the students. So how can they claim to have been impartial?

18. We didn't steal this stuff; we just liberated it from the bourgeois capitalist elite.

19. A: No, I don't think I should go out tonight. I take my studies very seriously, and I just *have* to get some work done tonight.

B: What makes you think that *I* don't take my studies seriously?

20. Senator Fisher has been a faithful spokesman for the state's manufacturing interests. It is not particularly surprising that, since his election twelve years ago, he has become one of the richest members of the state legislature.

II
Begging-the-Question
Fallacies

It is not uncommon to encounter an argument that uses its conclusion, usually in some subtle manner, as a part of the evidence in support of that very same conclusion. Such an argument is said to beg the question because it smuggles into the wording of one of the premises some form of the very claim the argument is designed to support. In such an argument, even though the conclusion is clearly not warranted by the evidence, the listener is, in effect, "begged" to accept it anyway. There is, of course, the appearance of evidential support; but at least a part of the "evidence" is really a form of the conclusion in disguise. Such arguments violate a rule of sound reasoning that one should employ as premises only those propositions that are self-evidently true or conclusions based upon other well-supported premises.

There are many different ways of arguing that could be characterized as question-begging. Some of the most common of these types of argument will be discussed in this chapter.

Circular Reasoning

Definition: This fallacy consists in either explicitly or implicitly assert-ing, in one of the premises of an argument, what is asserted in the conclusion of that argument.

The conclusion of a circular argument is literally used as one of its stated or unstated premises. However, when the conclusion appears as a premise, it is usually stated in different words or in a different form so that it is difficult to detect. Moreover, those who reason circularly rarely put their premises and conclusion close enough together to make detection simple. Indeed, an instance of circular reasoning is sometimes spread over the whole of an essay, a chapter, or even a book.

A circular argument may be formally valid, in the sense that the conclusion cannot be false if the premises are true; yet the argument is not at all capable of establishing the truth of the conclusion, for at least one of the premises is as doubtful as the conclusion. Hence, the premise in question can in no way support the conclusion. The circular argument, it could be said, only *pretends* to establish a claim. Once you have recognized the structure of a circular argument, you will see that it says nothing more significant than "A is true, because A is true."

Example: "Mr. Baker cannot be regarded as a competent music critic, because he is very biased. He is biased against all form of modern, especially atonal, music. I think that the reason he doesn't like modern music is that he is too uninformed to appreciate it; he simply doesn't have the qualities needed to make sound artistic judgments."

The circularity of this argument can be shown by pointing out its basic structure:

Baker is incompetent, because he is biased.

Baker is biased, because he doesn't like modern music.

Baker doesn't like modern music, because he is incompetent.

The claim that Baker is "uninformed," and without "the qualities needed to make sound artistic judgments" means the same thing as the claim that Baker is "incompetent." Hence, Baker's incompetence is given as a reason for his incompetence.

Example: One of the simplest and most easily detected forms of circular reasoning utilizes a single premise that is actually only a restatement of the conclusion in different words. Consider the following argument: "To use textbooks with profane and obscene words in them is immoral because it is not right for our children to hear vulgar, disrespectful, and ugly words." If you were to suggest that the argument is lacking in force because of the use of vague words such as *immoral* or *not right,* it could be shown that another set of words make the argument no less circular. Consider this new version of the argument: "To use textbooks with profane and obscene words in them is indefensible, because there are no good reasons for exposing our children to vulgar, disrespectful, and ugly words." In both versions, the argument has the form "A, because A."

Example: It is often the case that circular reasoning occurs as a result of nonexplicit assumptions. Suppose that Professor Hunt is defending the notion of determinism, the view that every event has a cause. As part of her proof she asks the following question concerning a particular event for which there is no apparent cause: "What could have produced it, if it were not a cause that brought it about?" In this case, the professor has implicitly assumed the position of determinism as a part of her proof, for the word *produced* in this context has the same meaning as *caused*. The form of the argument might look something like this:

Premise: Event X has no apparent cause.

Premise: If an event occurs, something must produce it.

Premise: Event X must be assumed to be produced.

Premise: *Produced* and *caused* are synonymous words.

Conclusion: Every event must be caused.

The circular character of this argument is now clear. The second premise is actually the conclusion in what is now not so good a disguise. Unfortunately, the position of determinism lends itself to circular reasoning, and it is not clear how it can be completely avoided. Yet if Professor Hunt wishes to establish her claim, she cannot do so by assuming as a part of the proof a position on the very question at issue, namely, whether determinism is true.

Attacking the Fallacy: If you are to avoid being misled by circular reasoning, it is necessary to keep a very keen eye on the logical structure of the argument in question. Make sure that no premise is simply an equivalent form of the conclusion or that no implicit or explicit premise assumes the truth of the conclusion. If the argument is a long one or one with a number of "chain links," carelessness in attention or a faulty memory may allow the sameness of premise and conclusion to go undetected.

You may directly attack circular reasoning by calling attention to the fact that the conclusion has already been assumed to be true as a part of the evidence. The fallacious character of circular reasoning might be demonstrated by an obvious or absurd instance of it. For instance, if you said, "Reading is fun, because it brings me lots of enjoyment," it should be clear that no claim has been established by such an argument. Yet it clearly has the same form as the more subtle examples given above, namely, "A because A." In most cases, circular arguers will agree that they assume the conclusion to be true because they are genuinely convinced of its truth. But such arguers need to be reminded that in an argument one's personal beliefs or convictions concerning the truth of a claim cannot be evidence for the truth of the same claim.

Question-Begging Expression

Definition: This fallacy consists in discussing an issue by means of terms that imply a position on the very question at issue. Typically, certain evaluative terms or phrases are used as if they were purely descriptive terms, in such a way as to direct the listener to a particular conclusion about a situation or issue. In other words, a value judgment is presented as if it were factual.

Such terms or phrases are question-begging insofar as they endorse, without appropriate evidence, a position on the very question at issue. Even though these expressions are not typically utilized as a part of an explicit argument, they have the function of leading to a particular conclusion. In such cases the listener is subtly being "begged" to infer a particular conclusion, although no good reasons are presented for doing so. The language of these expressions is usually emotionally charged and selected with a particular audience in mind.

Example: A U.S. Congressman recently sent a questionnaire to his constituents that included the question "Do you favor the give-away of the Panama Canal?" To include the expression *give-away* in such a question was very clearly an attempt to lead constituents to a particular conclusion on the issue of the Panama treaties.

Example: Often an allegedly objective analysis of an idea will end with an emotion-laden question-begging expression that has the effect of leading the listener, without evidence, to the speaker's conclusion. Consider a proposal before Congress that concludes with the comment "The whole idea smacks of socialism." Or suppose that a theologian describes another theologian's view as "dangerously close to pantheism." In each case, the speaker is attempting to lead the listener to reject the proposal in question because it leads to something presumably undesirable, although no reasons are given for its undesirability.

Example: Suppose that you are engaged in a discussion of the moral permissibility of abortion. One of the more important issues related to abortion is whether the fetus is to be considered a human being. If one of the discussants constantly refers to the fetus as *the baby*, he or she has begged the question on the very point at issue.

Attacking the Fallacy: Because a question-begging expression is not usually part of an explicit or formal argument, it is sometimes difficult to attack directly. Perhaps the best way to confront a person who has committed this fallacy is to point out those specific implicit assumptions that prevent a discussion of the issue from being an open one. Above all, do not be intimidated by the question-begger, particularly when he or she introduces a claim by such phrases as *obviously, any ten-year-old knows,* or *any fool knows.* This language suggests that the issue is not really an issue that deserves any further discussion or investigation. Such expressions function as defenses against attack, and if you wish not to be the victim of such tricks, you will risk the appearance of being naive, uninformed, or even mentally deficient by announcing, "Well, it's *not* obvious to me."

Loaded or Complex Question

Definition: This fallacy consists in formulating a question in a way that presupposes that a definite answer has already been given to some other, *unasked* question, or in treating a series of questions as if it involved only one question.

The complex question is, strictly speaking, not usually a fallacy found in arguments; it would be more accurate to describe it as an improper method of investigation. A respondent cannot answer a complex question without granting a questionable assumption or without giving the same answer to each of the two or more questions involved. Nearly all questions make some assumptions, but a question is not a complex one if the questioner has good reason to believe that the respondent would be quite willing to grant the assumption. An argument begs the question only when it forces the respondent to grant an assumption that is dubious or when it improperly assumes that the same answer will be given to each question in a series of questions.

Example: The most common form of this fallacy asks two questions, one of which is implicit and the other of which is explicit. Consider the young man who asks a fellow sophomore: "What fraternity are you going to pledge?" Or the pushy salesclerk who asks, "Cash or charge?" long before you have decided to buy the merchandise. Or even the worried mother who asks her bachelor son: "When are you going to settle down and get married?" In each case, the questioner has given a positive answer to the implicit question: namely, that the sophomore has decided to pledge some fraternity, that the customer has decided to buy the merchandise, and that the bachelor has concluded that some day he will get married. Apart from appropriate evidence, a positive answer to each of these questions is unwarranted.

Example: In a different version of the complex question a series of questions is treated as if it involved only one question. Suppose that I am asked: "Are you and Nancy going to the wedding and the reception afterward at the country club?" This question actually involves at least three different questions: It asks if I am going to the wedding, if I am going to the reception, and if my wife, Nancy, will be my companion at these events.[1] It might be the case that I would wish to answer positively in response to two of the three questions but negatively in response to the third. Yet the question is asked in such a way that only one answer can be given. If I do not insist that the question be divided, the questionable assumption that is granted to the questioner is that the same answer will be given to each of the questions.

Example: "Why is it that the children of divorce are emotionally more unstable than those children raised in unbroken homes?" This is a complex question, for the questioner has assumed a position on a questionable claim, namely, that children of divorce are emotionally more unstable than those children raised in unbroken homes. That claim must be established before the question calling for an explanation of such a phenomenon can be appropriately asked. Indeed, if the substantive claim can be shown to be false, the call for explanation would be out of order. However, as it was originally asked, the question does not consider

[1]It could conceivably be an even more complex question, for it could be further divided by asking if Nancy were going to accompany me to the wedding and if she were going to accompany me to the reception. Indeed, a careful analysis of the original question might reveal at least sixteen different questions if all possible combinations involving the four variables were considered.

the possibility that the substantive claim may be false. Hence, the respondent is "begged" to grant the truth of that assumption.

Attacking the Fallacy: There are a number of ways you might respond to a complex question. First, refuse to give a straightforward *yes* or *no* to such a question. Second, point out the questionable assumption and deal with it directly. Third, insist, if necessary, that the question be appropriately divided, so that each question can be answered separately. Remember that even standard rules of parliamentary procedure provide for "dividing the question"; indeed, a motion to divide the question has a priority status.

If you yourself are accused of asking a loaded question, make sure that your accuser is using the term *loaded* correctly. Sometimes when people do not want to answer a question because their answer might be personally embarrassing, they will accuse the questioner of asking a loaded question. In logic, however, a question is not loaded unless it contains an unwarranted assumption. There is nothing fallacious about asking a question the answer to which might be personally embarrassing to the respondent.

Leading Question

Definition: This fallacy consists in "planting" a proposed answer to a question at issue by the manner in which the question is asked.

The leading question, like the complex question, is not a fallacy found in arguments; it too is better described as an inappropriate procedure in inquiry. However, the procedure of the leading question usually involves asking only *one* question. This question contains an unsupported claim, in that it unjustifiably assumes a position on what is probably a debatable, or at least an open, issue. Furthermore, the questioner is, in effect, asking another to assume the same position on the issue yet fails to provide any adequate justification for the respondent to do so. The questioner is therefore simply "begging" the respondent to give the desired answer.

Example: Suppose that a long-time friendship between two people is seriously threatened with dissolution because one of the friends has committed an act that the other considers very "unfriendlike" in character. The perpetrator of the act asks: "Our friendship will never die over something as trivial as this, will it?" The questioner has assumed that the matter in question is a trivial one, and is begging the friend to accept it as trivial, when the triviality or nontriviality of the act is the very question at issue.

Example: Consider the courtroom lawyer who leads her client in the following manner: "You *did* plan to return the money that you borrowed from the cash drawer, did you not?" In this case the defense lawyer is "leading" the witness, by assuming a position on the very question at issue—namely, whether the defendant embezzled the money or whether he inappropriately "borrowed" it. Even though the lawyer may be convinced that it was simply borrowed, that is, that her client is innocent, a proper procedure for getting at the truth of the matter would be to encourage the witness to explain the circumstances related to the taking of the money. This would be information relevant to the conclusion finally reached, that is, that the money was simply borrowed. In this way the claim of the defense would more likely be a supported one. Planting a proposed answer is not only likely to be disallowed by the judge, it is also a procedure that is likely to weaken the case for the defense.

Example: Suppose a faculty member approaches one of his friends just before a faculty meeting at which a vote on an important curricular matter is to be taken and asks: "I don't suppose you would turn your back on your friends by voting against us on this issue, would you?" The questioner here is making an unsupported or questionable claim, which he is "begging" the friend to accept—namely, that voting on the other side of the issue is equivalent to being a traitor or unfriendlike. The questioner begs the question by telling the respondent how to answer without explaining how voting in accordance with one's own convictions is a traitorous act. A proper approach to such a situation would be to give the friend some good reasons for the superiority of his position. Such a procedure would probably also be more successful; it might gain the support of the friend on the issue in question.

Attacking the Fallacy: To confront the leading question tactic, you must find some way to reveal to the questioner that he or she is asking you to grant an assumption that is at least part of the very question at issue. When that issue is clear, you might point out that you think the position you are asked to adopt requires more evidential support than it now has, or at least that you are not now willing to give the questioner's "begged-for" answer on the basis of the available evidence. Of course, if the position held by the questioner seems self-evidently true or is one you find well supported, then from your perspective no fallacy has really been committed.

Question-Begging Definition

Definition: This fallacy consists in attempting to establish an irrefutable position in an argument by means of a questionable definition. What appears to be a factual or empirical claim is often rendered impervious to counterevidence by being subtly, and sometimes unconsciously, interpreted by the claimant as a definitional statement. The claim at issue thereby becomes "true" by definition.

The question-begging definition begs the question at issue because it settles an allegedly empirical question by virtue of the definition of a key term.[2] A clue that such a deceptive technique is being used could be the presence of such modifying words as *truly, really, essentially,* or *genuinely* before the key term in the discussion of an issue. Even though the speaker may strongly believe that such a term

[2]An empirical question is one that is capable of being verified or falsified (disproved) by observation or experiment

should be defined in the way that he or she has done it, if the very definition of a key term has the effect of settling a controversial empirical claim, then the fallacy of question-begging definition has been committed.

Example: Suppose that Paul maintains the empirical claim that *true* love never ends in separation or divorce. When he is presented with examples of true love followed by divorce, he insists that such cases were not *genuine* cases of true love. His "evidence" that they were not cases of true love is that they ended in divorce. Paul is hereby settling the issue by definition, for his judgment is that any marriage that ends in divorce could not have been a case of true love. No evidence is allowed to count against his claim. If Paul wishes to define *true love* as love that would not end in separation, that is his prerogative, although such a definition is a questionable one from the perspective of ordinary language. However, Paul's claim has the appearance of being a factual assertion, and factual assertions are assertions for which empirical evidence is relevant. If Paul had intended his claim to be a definitional one, he should have made that clear from the beginning. It is often the case, however, that a claimant is simply confused about the character of the claim. It is only when counterevidence is presented that the claimant reinterprets the seemingly empirical claim as a definitional one.

Example: When former New York City Mayor John Lindsay switched from the Republican Party to the Democratic Party several years ago, a number of his critics, especially Republicans, claimed that he had obviously not been a "true-blue" Republican or he wouldn't have switched political parties. The primary "evidence" the critics could cite for Lindsay's "non-true-blue" Republicanism was that he switched parties. It was obvious that little evidence would have been allowed to count against the claim. This is, therefore, a case of the fallacy of question-begging definition; for the *definition* of a "true-blue" Republican is apparently one who would never leave the Republican Party. Hence, the only matter that is disputable is whether the definition is an appropriate one; there is no empirical claim at issue.

Example: Several years ago, in an effort to defend the relevance of philosophy to the students in my introductory philosophy course, I announced that "all philosophical questions are answerable." To emphasize my point, I added that it was unlikely that I, a professor of philosophy, would have taken upon myself the lifetime task of studying philosophical questions if I thought they were inherently unsolvable. I claimed that if a "philosophical question" were such that there were no realistic possibility of solving it, then it wasn't really a philosophical question.

When an alert student pointed out the question-begging character of my claim, I then had to admit that I *defined* a philosophical question as one that has the possibility of being answered. It then became clear to me and to my students that I was not at all making an empirical claim about all the philosophical questions that I had encountered; I was simply explaining how I was using the term *philosophical question*.

Attacking the Fallacy: If you suspect a question-begging definition, ask the speaker directly what kind of statement he or she is making. If the speaker is puzzled by your question, it might be necessary to explain, as simply as possible, the difference between a definitional and an empirical claim. If the claim is found to be definitional, it is obviously not subject to falsification, although the speaker should be prepared to defend the definition against alternative definitions based on ordinary language or the thinking of relevant authorities. If the claim is found to be empirical, then empirical data are relevant and the claimant should be open to the possibility of counterevidence.

Apriorism

Definition: This fallacy consists in refusing to look at any evidence that might count against one's claim or assumption. An extension of this fallacy consists in being unwilling or unable to specify any conceivable evidence that might possibly count against one's claim.

When people argue in an a priori way—that is, in deliberate disregard of the evidence or in advance of the facts—it is usually because they have a very firm belief regarding the matter in question or hold firmly to some principle or assumption from which a prediction is being made or from which a conclusion is being deduced. Yet any method of thinking that allows clinging blindly to empirical claims or to assumptions from which such claims may be deduced, without proper attention to relevant evidence, is obstructive to the task of discovering the truth. Indeed, such a pattern of thinking violates a methodological postulate of empirical thinking, namely, that every nondefinitional claim has the inherent possibility of being false.

People who commit the fallacy of apriorism are saying in effect that counterevidence is not relevant to their claim. Yet if counterevidence is not relevant to the claim, it would seem to follow logically that supportive evidence would be just as irrelevant. Just as it would be absurd to take an opinion poll and record only the positive responses, it is similarly absurd to disregard evidence that tends to falsify (or weaken) a particular empirical claim and to utilize only that evidence in support of it.

Example: Suppose that a college freshman is discussing with his mother the possible legalization of marijuana. As a part of the discussion, the student calls attention to a number of recent government studies concerning marijuana use. These reports conclude that there is no strong evidence to suggest that moderate use of marijuana is in any way harmful. The mother retorts: "I don't care what the conclusions of your so-called government studies or any other studies are. Marijuana is obviously harmful and should not be legalized under any circumstances." There is apparently no evidence that she would accept as weakening her position. Indeed, if the student were to ask her directly if there were *any* evidence that she might accept, she would probably reply: "Nothing could convince me that I am wrong."

Example: "I couldn't care less what is in your biology textbook. I know that I didn't come from some monkey or lower form of life or whatever you call it. The Bible says that God created man in his own image. And unlike the Bible, your textbook was written by a mere human being. What's in those textbooks is just somebody's opinion." It is clear that there is no evidence that could convince such a person on the matter of biological evolution, as any evidence offered would have been marshaled by a "mere human being." Further discussion of the issue would seem to be a waste of mental energy.

Example: Consider this conversation that I had several years ago concerning the relative merits of the Democratic and Republican Parties. My opponent claimed that, unlike the Republican Party, the Democratic Party had a long history of crooked deals, scandals, and "closet skeletons." I quickly called her attention to the then-recent break-in of the Democratic Party Headquarters at Watergate by people hired by the Committee to Re-elect the President (Nixon). To my surprise, she countered: "Those people weren't hired by the Republicans. The Democrats couldn't get anything on Nixon, so they hired some people to break into their own headquarters so they could put the blame on Nixon and the Republicans." I didn't respond. She was so convinced of the moral purity of the Republican Party that I was certain that she would ignore or "rationalize away" *any* counterevidence that I might offer.[3]

Attacking the Fallacy: To demonstrate whether your verbal opponent is genuinely open to counterevidence, you could ask what particular kind of evidence, if it could be produced, might seriously weaken the claim. If the claimant cannot or will not specify such evidence, then there is probably no possibility of altering his or her opinion, and you would be wise to refuse to discuss the issue further. Indeed, it might be helpful to point out to your opponent the fruitlessness of discussing something with someone who will entertain no counterevidence nor admit to even the possibility of being wrong. In such a case, it would be more productive and less frustrating to move the discussion to some other issue.

If you can get your opponent to listen to counterevidence, ask him or her to respond to it or to evaluate it. If your opponent refuses to listen or respond, the a priori character of such thinking should become clearly evident to all. If your opponent complies with your request, seriously and without rationalizing, the fallacy of apriorism will no longer be a problem, and the discussion will have moved to the substantive claim at issue.

Exercises

A. Identify the type of begging-the-question in each of the following:

1. Mr. St. Clair says to his nephew David, who is a high school senior: "Where will you be going to college next year, David?"

2. A: The criminal mind simply cannot be rehabilitated.

[3]Rationalization is briefly discussed in Chapter III, p. 45.

B: That's not true. I know several criminals who have been completely rehabilitated.

A: Well, then, those people must not have been real criminals.

3. It's supposed to be in the low twenties tonight, so surely we're not going to the football game, are we?

4. A: But how do you know that the Bible is actually divinely inspired?

B: Because it says right in the third chapter of II Timothy that "all Scripture is given by inspiration of God."

5. I don't care *what* the report of the President's Commission on Obscenity and Pornography says. I know that the viewing of pornographic materials does encourage people to commit sex crimes. The first step in controlling such crimes is to clamp down on the pornographers.

6. Surely no one in his right mind would join up with the lunatic supporters of the so-called Equal Rights Amendment.

7. A: Only the fittest of organisms survive.

B: How do you know?

A: Well, if they survive, they must be fit.

B: Yes, but how do you know that it is only the most fit of the organisms that survive?

A: Those creatures who have survived obviously have survived because they are somehow adapted for survival.

8. Why should the President set up a commission to find out the causes of poverty in the United States? *I* can tell you what causes it. It's just laziness! That's all it is!

9. A: Man is a creature of despair. In order to be genuinely authentic, human beings must experience some despair.

B: But I don't ever have such experiences. I really don't. I think you are wrong.

A: Well, obviously you are simply deceiving yourself if you never allow such feelings of despair to come to full consciousness. Being a creature of despair is what distinguishes humans from nonhumans.

10. Cynthia, do you really want me to have to sit through another one of those horrible P.T.A. meetings tonight?

B. From among all the fallacies studied to this point, choose the fallacy that most closely resembles the problem exhibited in each of the following:

11. Steve would never kill anyone. I *know* my boy. He was always polite and thoughtful. We raised him right. He went to church with us every Sunday. No matter what the evidence says, I *know* he didn't murder anybody.

12. Professor: "Unless someone wishes to add anything further to the discussion of this absurd issue, I suggest that we move on to the next topic."

13. A: I just don't understand what could have happened to the $50.00 that I had in my desk drawer.

B: Why don't you ask Denise? She's been out shopping all day today. She just came back with a whole bunch of new stuff. She's in her room now, I think.

14. One of Senator Fisher's constituents asks: "Are you going to vote for the proposed cut in the defense budget—a cut that will surely weaken our military posture around the world?"

15. **A:** A Christian would never drink alcoholic beverages.

B: That's just not true. I know several Christians who occasionally take a drink. In fact, I know some Christian ministers who do.

A: Then as far as I'm concerned, they couldn't be real Christians.

16. Diana, did you empty the dishwasher and clean the kitchen while I was gone, as I asked you?

17. The faculty is supposed to vote next week on the committee's newest "hodge-podge" curricular proposal.

18. I wasn't eavesdropping. Really! I was merely listening to see whom you were talking to.

19. Sign on theater marquee: "Family entertainment every night except Tuesday."

20. **Steve:** If Ben doesn't stop harassing me, I'm going to bust his head in.

Mark (speaking to Ben later): Steve said that he was going to bust your head in.

III
Unwarranted Assumption Fallacies

The patterns of argument discussed in this chapter are fallacious because they are based upon questionable, although sometimes popular, principles or assumptions. Although it is not my purpose to account for the *evolution* of bad thinking, it is probably the case that many of these assumptions are a part of our conventional wisdom because they seem to have a "ring of truth" about them, or they may even *be* true in some contexts. However, no conclusion would be warranted if it were based on merely the assumed truth of any of these principles. Moreover, any *argument* based simply upon such assumptions must be regarded as fallacious even if its conclusion happens to be true.

Fallacy of the Continuum

Definition: This fallacy consists in assuming that small differences are always unimportant or that supposed contraries, as long as they are connected by intermediate small differences, are really very much the same. Hence, there is the failure to recognize the importance or necessity of sometimes making what might appear to be arbitrary distinctions or cut-off points.

The assumption involved in this fallacy is a very common one, and it is not easy to persuade people of its dubious character. This assumption is expressed in the common claim that "it's only a matter of degree." This "only a matter of degree" kind of thinking implicitly claims that small differences are unimportant or that making definite distinctions between things on a continuum is almost impossible, or at least arbitrary. A more graphic name for this fallacy might be the camel's back fallacy as in "One more straw won't break the camel's back." Anyone who has played the child's game "the last straw" knows that one more straw *can* break the camel's back. The game rules specify that each player be given a handful of very lightweight wooden "straws." Then each player in turn places a single straw in a basket on the camel's back. The player who places the straw that breaks the camel's back, that is, causes it to collapse, loses the game. There *is* a straw that makes the difference between the camel's back breaking and not breaking. Similarly, there is a distinction that can be made on a continuum between one category and its contrary.

Nevertheless, clear distinctions between these categories are sometimes very difficult to make. Vague words particularly lend themselves to this difficulty. At what point, for example, does a warm evening become a cool one or a boy become a man? The fallacy of the continuum is not committed by those who fail to make these precise distinctions but by those who assume that such distinctions cannot be made. There *is* a difference between a warm evening and a cool evening just as there is a difference between a boy and a man. To make distinctions may in some cases seem somewhat arbitrary, but it is appropriate that some distinctions be made. At any rate, it would be fallacious to assume in one's thinking that such distinctions could not be made.

The ancient name of this fallacy is the fallacy of the beard. Such a name probably originated in the context of the ancient practice of debating such a question as "How many hairs would one have to have in order to have a beard?" We would be reluctant—because it would appear arbitrary—to specify a certain number of hairs, but obviously there is a difference between having a beard and not having a beard. Is there not a cut-off point between the two? Another graphic label sometimes attached to this fallacy is the slippery slope. As the name suggests, when we grant that one small difference is unimportant, we find ourselves slipping on down the slope to the next little difference and so on. It appears that there is no place to dig in and stop the sliding once we take that first step over the edge. The slippery slope image suggests that if we are justified in taking one small step in a particular direction, additional steps are justified also; for there seems to be no good reason to stop or dig in at any particular point. Nevertheless, to avoid the fallacy of the continuum, we must develop criteria for imposing appropriate stopping points.

Example: Arguments utilizing the assumption involved in the fallacy of the continuum are very persuasive. Indeed, even students who have carefully studied the fallacy have been heard to argue in the following manner: "Professor Morris added five points to every student's final numerical average. It seems to me that if he added five points, he could have gone on and added six points. Then I would have passed the course. After all, there is very little difference between five points and six points. Yet that one point made the difference between passing and failing the course. Ben Sanders had a 60 average after the five-point addition and I had a 59. He passed and I didn't; but does he really know that much more philosophy than I?" It is probably the case that the student with the 59 average did not know that much less philosophy than the student with the 60 average; but some cut-off point has to be established in order to avoid a slippery slope that could make extremes—for example, knowing and not knowing philosophy—indistinguishable.

Example: A number of people have sometimes been convinced by a clever salesclerk that a little larger monthly payment isn't going to make very much difference:

Customer: I just can't afford that much for an air conditioner right now.
Salesclerk: Why don't you just put it on your charge account?
Customer: But the monthly payment on my account is already eighty dollars a month.
Salesclerk: But if you buy the air conditioner now, you can have it all summer, when you really need it, and it will only add twenty dollars a month to your payment.

Such reasoning, if it leads one to a purchase, need occur only a few times before the customer might be in serious financial difficulty.

Example: What person on a diet or trying to cut down on smoking has not been deceived by the argument that one little doughnut or one more cigarette surely can't make any real difference?

Attacking the Fallacy: If there are any doubts about whether the fallacy of the continuum is really a fallacy, ask your verbal opponent for the definition of some vague term such as *rich person*. Try to get him or her to be very specific about the amount of assets in dollars that a person would have to have in order to qualify as *rich*. Let us call that amount X. Then subtract a small amount, for example, ten dollars, from that number and ask if a person having X minus ten dollars would still be rich. Your opponent will no doubt say "yes." Repeat the question again and again, subtracting a few more dollars each time. Your opponent will probably continue to answer "yes" every time until it becomes clear that you have been able to place him or her on a slippery slope because of the fallacious assumption that small differences are unimportant. If your opponent does not become conscious of such fallacious reasoning, he or she will soon be assenting to the claim that a person having X minus X dollars is rich, which is absurd.

It would be naive to deny that making distinctions is sometimes very difficult; but at the same time it should be insisted upon that distinctions can and sometimes must be made. For example, there must be a difference between failing and passing a course and between staying on a diet and not staying on a diet. Moreover, hot and cold are discernible distinctions, even though hot and cold are extreme points separated on a continuum by a large number of small intermediate differences. Surely you would not wish to say that a hot day is really not much different from a cold day because "it's only a matter of degree."

Fallacy of Composition

Definition: This fallacy consists in assuming that, because a property is affirmed or denied of the parts of some whole, that same property may also be affirmed or denied of the whole.

The fallacy of composition is committed principally in those cases where a "whole," because of the particular relationship of its parts, represents something different from simply the sum or the combination of those parts. In such cases, the whole either takes on a new characteristic because of its composition, or at least does not take on or maintain particular characteristics attributed to each of its parts. The fallacy, then, is to attribute to the whole those characteristics that are attributed to each of the parts making up that whole, simply because it is a whole made up of those parts. A person who commits such a fallacy has ignored or failed to understand that the way the parts relate, interact, or affect each other often changes the character of the whole. For example, the fact that each of the players on a football team is an excellent player would not be a sufficient reason to infer that the football team is an excellent one.

This fallacy is often confused with the fallacy of insufficient sample or unrepresentative statistics, wherein we infer something about a whole class of things on the basis of one or a few instances of that thing.[1] For example, we might infer on the basis of our several bad experiences with Chevrolets that all Chevrolets are inferior automobiles. In this case we are inferring something about a class of things on the basis of one or only a few instances of that thing. The fallacy of composition, however, is committed when we infer something about the characteristic of the whole because of some characteristic of *all* of its parts.

Example: If we were to infer that the United States is a strong and efficient country because each of the fifty states is strong and efficient, it would be a clear case of the fallacy of composition. In fact, the strength or efficiency of each of the states might suggest that each state has a kind of independence that would detract from the possibility of a strong and efficient nation. In such a case, the whole might not take on the characteristics of its parts.

Example: Who has not heard this fallacy committed in the most casual comments? "Dan is a fine young man; Becky's a fine young woman. They'll make a lovely couple." The whole called *marriage* is more than a sum of the parts that make it up. Hence, the parts, by virtue of their relationship in the marital whole, might create something very much lacking in loveliness or fineness.

Example: It is often quite hard to recognize the subtlety of the fallacy of composition. I have often heard comments like the following: "Professor Denham and Professor Carruth are going to team-teach a course next spring in the philosophy of science. They are two of our best teachers, so it really ought to be a good course." If Professors Denham and Carruth are good teachers in the sense that term is ordinarily used in an academic context, it could very likely be the case that the team-taught course would be a poor one. Many "good" teachers are good by virtue of their total and singular control of the classroom. A team-taught course usually does not allow for such control. There could also be other reasons, of course, why the professors might not work well together. Assuming that they will is falling into the fallacy of composition.

[1]See Chapter IX, pp. 109–112.

Attacking the Fallacy: A careful attempt should be made to show the person who commits this fallacy just *how* a whole may very well represent something different from simply the sum of its parts. Try an *obvious* example: If it is the case that Diana has a very pretty blouse, a pretty skirt, and pretty shoes, they will not necessarily make a beautiful outfit together. The clash of patterns or colors could render the outfit quite ugly. However, it is important to keep in mind that wholes are not *always* different in character from their parts. For example, if every cup of punch in the punch bowl is sour, it would be entirely warranted to draw the conclusion that all the punch in the punch bowl is sour. In this case, there is nothing about a cup of this punch that, when it was mixed with all the other cups of punch, would change the taste or character of the whole bowl of punch.

Furthermore, in some cases *some* evidence for a claim about a whole *is* provided by facts about the parts. For an "attack" strategy, then, you might say to your opponent that you understand why he or she might have drawn a conclusion about a characteristic of the whole based upon a characteristic of the parts, for in some cases the parts *do* provide evidence for a claim about the whole. At the same time, you might use a few examples to illustrate how such an understandable assumption can lead to absurd conclusions in other cases. The problem lies in assuming that a characteristic *automatically* passes over to a whole from the parts.

Fallacy of Division

Definition: This fallacy consists in assuming that, because a property is affirmed or denied of some whole, that same property may be affirmed or denied of any of the parts of that whole.

One form of the fallacy of division is the opposite of the fallacy of composition. Rather than assuming that a characteristic of the parts is also a characteristic of the whole, it assumes that a characteristic of the whole is also a characteristic of each of the parts. However, as we have seen, under certain conditions a whole represents something quite different from simply the sum or the combination of its parts.

A second form of the fallacy of division occurs when we infer something about a member of a class on the basis of a *generalization* about the whole class. In this case, the characteristic of the whole should not be applied to the parts, because the characteristic of the whole is only a statistical generalization based on the characteristics of *most* of the parts. Such a characteristic of the class *is* attributable to many of its parts; but as it is impossible to know to which members of the class the generalization may apply, it would be fallacious to assume, without additional evidence, that the characteristic accurately describes any particular member of the class.

Example: The following example will illustrate the first form of the fallacy of division: It may be true that John has a handsome face; yet it may not be true that any part of his face, for example, the nose or the mouth, is handsome apart from the rest of his face. In this case, a characteristic of the whole is not necessarily a characteristic of the parts.

Example: Although normal human beings are conscious entities, we should not infer from such a characteristic of the whole that individual cells or molecules of that whole are conscious entities.

Example: Suppose that a high school senior rejected the idea of attending a large university on the grounds that he or she preferred small, intimate classes. To think in this way would be to commit the fallacy of division, for the student could not infer that a large university would have only large classes. Even if it were statistically true that large universities usually have large classes, the student could not legitimately infer that any *particular* class in the university would be large. The first form of the fallacy of division is seen in the inference drawn from large universities to large classes. The second form of the fallacy of division would be seen in an inference about the size of a particular university class drawn from a statistical generalization about the size of classes in large universities.

Attacking the Fallacy: The attack upon the first form of fallacy of division is similar to the attack upon the fallacy of composition. Say to your opponent that you understand why he or she might have drawn a conclusion about a characteristic of the parts based on a characteristic of the whole, because in *some* cases evidence for a claim about the parts *is* provided by facts about the whole. Then you might use a few examples to demonstrate how such an understandable assumption could lead to absurd conclusions in some cases. For example, you might point out how absurd it would be to assume that a particular state is diversified in terms of its climate or industry simply because it is a part of the United States, which is so diversified.

This example might seal the case against the second form of the fallacy of division: If it is statistically the case that Maytag washing machines do not break down during their first three years of use, it would be absurd to exclude the possibility that your *particular* Maytag machine might break down during its first three years.

False Alternatives

Definition: This fallacy consists in assuming too few alternatives and at the same time assuming that one of the suggested alternatives must be true.

Because a reduction in the number of alternatives often results in only two extreme alternatives being presented, this fallacy is sometimes referred to as the black-and-white fallacy. Thinking in such extremes requires much less mental effort than looking diligently for all possible solutions to a problem. The fallacy of false alternatives, however, is not thinking in extremes; it is oversimplifying the problem situation by failing to entertain or at least to recognize all its plausible alternative solutions.

A common form of the fallacy of false alternatives derives from the failure to differentiate properly between contradictories (negatives) and contraries (opposites). Contradictories exclude any gradations between their extremes; there is no middle ground between a term and its negative, for example, between *hot* and *not hot*. Contraries, on the other hand, allow a number of gradations between their extremes; there is plenty of middle ground between a term and its opposite, for example, between *hot* and *cold*. The problem is that contraries are often treated as if they were contradictories. In the case of contradictories (a term and its negative), one of the two extremes must be true and the other false: It is either hot or it is not hot. In the case of contraries (a term and its opposite), it is possible for both extremes to be false: It could be neither hot nor cold. To assume that it must be either hot or cold would be to treat contraries as if they were contradictories and thereby commit the fallacy of false alternatives.

Example: A case of treating contraries as if they were contradictories is seen in one of the well-known sayings of Jesus: "If you are not for me, you must be against me." A similar instance may be found in the claim that if one is not a theist, then one must be an atheist. Neither claim seems to allow for the alternative of neutrality (or agnosticism).

Example: One would clearly commit the fallacy of false alternatives by assuming that a particular political candidate was running on the Democratic ticket simply because she was not running on the Republican ticket. There are a number of alternative tickets on which one might run, or one could be running on no ticket at all.

Example: Suppose that Professor Morton insists that a certain activity is either morally right or morally wrong. If *morally right* means morally obligatory and *morally wrong* means morally prohibited, then the fallacy of false alternatives has been committed, because there may be other alternatives. One such alternative might be to treat the activity as morally permissible. The terms, *right* and *wrong*, then, must be regarded as opposites rather than as contradictories.

Example: Absolutistic thinking or thinking in extremes is quite frequently found in political rhetoric. The issue of so-called socialized medicine is often presented in terms of false alternatives: "Either we allow the government to take total control of the field of medicine or we must allow our doctors to be free of governmental restrictions." Surely there are a number of middle ground alternatives to the problem of medical care.

Attacking the Fallacy: Genuine "either-or" situations are very rare. If you are presented with one, it probably would be a good idea to treat it with a bit of skepticism—unless, of course, the either-or is a set of contradictories. In almost all other cases, more than two alternatives are usually available, although those additional alternatives might have been ignored by the arguer. As a means of attacking an argument based on limited alternatives, point out a number of other alternatives and challenge the arguer to show why they do not qualify as plausible solutions. Once all the plausible alternatives have been considered, then the question becomes that of determining which of the plausible alternatives is best supported by the evidence or by good reasons.

Is-Ought Fallacy

Definition: This fallacy consists in assuming that because something *is* the case, it *ought* to be the case. Likewise, it consists in assuming that because something *is not* the case, it *ought not* to be the case.

The is-ought fallacy is permeated by moral or value overtones. The "way things are" is regarded as ideal or morally proper simply because "things" are as they are. No good reasons are given for the appropriateness of a thing's being the way it is; it is simply assumed that if it *is*, it must be right, and the possibility of changing it is not seriously entertained.

This fallacy can easily be confused with the appeal to tradition.[2] However, in the case of the is-ought fallacy, it is argued that the status quo should be maintained not out of reverence for the past, as is the case with the fallacious appeal to tradition, but simply because it is the status quo. It is assumed that if it is the status quo, then there is sufficient reason for it to be appropriate.

The is-ought fallacy can also be confused with the fallacious appeal to public opinion.[3] The appeal to public opinion is usually used in an attempt to establish the truth of opinions; that is, an opinion or judgment is erroneously assumed to be true because it is held by a large number of people. The is-ought fallacy, however, is used to establish the rightness or appropriateness of a particular kind of behavior or situation, simply because it is presently engaged in by a large number of people. Although in practice the two may be confused, I suggest that the appeal to public opinion be understood as a faulty method of establishing what *is* the case, and the is-ought fallacy be understood as a faulty method of establishing what *ought* to be the case.

Example: "Smoking marijuana is illegal, son! If there were nothing wrong with it, it wouldn't be illegal, don't you understand?" The fact that marijuana is illegal constitutes no reason whatsoever for the propriety of that status. In other words, there is no logical justification for claiming that because it *is* illegal, it *ought* to be illegal.

Example: "Public school teachers and professors should not seek to engage in collective bargaining. After all, very few teachers are presently involved in such practices. There is simply very little interest in that sort of thing in our profession." The fact that very few teachers are currently members of labor unions is not a sufficient reason for concluding that such involvement is inappropriate.

Example:

Professor Taylor: Students should be allowed to be more involved in the decision-making processes at this school.

[2]See Chapter VII, pp. 92–93.
[3]See Chapter VII, pp. 95–96.

Professor Smith: The fact is that a college is just not very demo-cratic in character. So let's not tamper with the governmental structure. Let's concentrate on some other important things that need our attention.

Professor Smith does not even entertain the possibility of introduc-ing more democracy into the institutional structure, simply because of the "way things are."

Attacking the Fallacy: An argument always requires evidence or good reasons to support its conclusion. If no evidence or reason is given other than the status quo, you should point out that fact and insist that some specific evidence or reasons be provided. If the arguer is able to provide such support, you can then evaluate the support in order to determine the soundness of the argument. For example, the fact that people are being discriminated against because of their sex is not a good reason for sex discrimination. However, if there are weighty reasons for treating people differently on the basis of their sex, then sex discrimination might indeed be regarded as appropriate behavior.

Wishful Thinking

Definition: This fallacy consists in assuming that because one *wants* something to be the case, it *is* or *will be* the case.

A strong desire that a claim be true often leads us to the conclusion that it really is true. We sometimes want something to be true so strongly that we actually believe that it *is* or *will be* the case. Indeed, sometimes we so much desire that a claim be true or that a course of action be acceptable, that false yet plausible-sounding reasons are used to justify the claim or action. This kind of thinking is sometimes referred to as *rationalization*. Many weak arguments, of course, could be interpreted as cases of wishful thinking, because presumably the arguer *wants* his or her conclusion to be true. However, the term *wishful thinking* should be reserved for those patterns of reasoning which explicitly derive conclusions from desires or wishes. Rationalization, then, would *not* be a case of wishful thinking, although it is no doubt motivated by a strong interest in a certain conclusion.

There is a sense in which the fallacy of wishful thinking could be regarded as the opposite of the is-ought fallacy. This would make it the "ought-is" fallacy. Rather than assuming that what *is* the case, *ought* to be the case, the wishful thinker assumes that what *ought* (or is wanted) to be the case, *is* the case. However, as we have seen, the inference from *ought* (want) to *is* works no better than *is* to *ought*. Our feelings or emotions are ordinarily irrelevant to the truth of a claim or the soundness of an argument. Hence, a desire that a particular conclusion be true usually constitutes no evidence in support of that claim.

Example: One of the more serious arguments for life after death put forth by a British theologian goes like this: "There must be a life after death, because almost all people desire it. It is a part of the very nature of human beings to desire it. If there were no life after death, then why would all humans desire it? Like the desires for food, water, and sex, all of which are satiable, the desire for life after death is universal." Even if the claim about the universality of the desire for the afterlife is true, it is quite conceivable that a universal desire could go totally unsatisfied. Consider, if you will, the desire of most of us to have more money than we presently have. Wanting something to be the case, even if it is universally wanted, does not make it so.

Example: It is desired by a number of young people that the sale and use of marijuana be legalized. However, if we assume on such grounds that it *will* be legalized, we will assuredly be guilty of the fallacy of wishful thinking. It is true, of course, that the wishes of a legislator's constituents often influence his or her action; but such desires alone are not sufficient grounds for believing that particular legislative actions will be taken.

Example: Consider the time you were kind enough to cat-sit in your own home with your neighbor's cat. When you returned to the living room after a short absence, you noticed that your goldfish had disappeared. The neighbor's explanation: "Boots couldn't have done that; he's just not that kind of cat. The goldfish probably jumped out onto the floor somehow." Your neighbor probably wished so badly that Boots was not responsible for the dastardly deed that he clearly gave more weight to his own argument or explanation than it may have deserved.

Attacking the Fallacy: One method of attacking the fallacy of wishful thinking would be to offer strong evidence for a claim that is contrary to the claim at issue and to ask your opponent to evaluate that evidence. Another method might be to ask your opponent if the argument and "evidence" would be evaluated in the same way if he or she wished the claim to be false. Finally, you might ask your opponent if his or her thinking is any different from believing that it will not rain tomorrow simply because a picnic is planned; that is, because one does not *want* it to rain.

Misuse of a Generalization

Definition: This fallacy consists in assuming that a generalization or principle has no exceptions and thus misapplying it in a particular instance. Conversely, it consists in attempting to refute a generalization by means of exceptional cases.

One who commits this particular fallacy overlooks the fact that there are usually implicit qualifications of almost any generalization, rule, or principle, that render it inapplicable in some unusual cases. The fallacy occurs when one assumes that a generalization can be applied in *every* case, no matter what the circumstances are, or when one assumes that unusual or exceptional cases would falsify or refute such generalizations. It should be noted, however, that exceptions, or so-called accidental circumstances, are quite different from genuine counterexamples to a generalization. A counterexample may indeed falsify a principle, but it should not require special or unusual circumstances to do so. If there are genuine counterexamples to the principle, it is probably the case that the generalization is ill-conceived or based on an insufficient sample or unrepresentative statistics.[4] Because this fallacy involves the problem of unusual or accidental circumstances, it is often referred to as the fallacy of accident, and its converse is referred to as the fallacy of converse accident.

Example: A general principle to which most of us subscribe is that people are entitled to use their own property in whatever way they wish. But it would be a misapplication of this principle to say that no restrictions should be imposed, for example, upon the driving of one's own automobile while intoxicated. Intoxication is a special circumstance in which the general principle is inapplicable because of the serious potential harm to others.

Example: If the principle with regard to X-rated movies shown at drive-in theaters is that "no one under eighteen will be allowed into the theater," it would be a misapplication of this rule for an attendant to refuse to allow a couple to bring their infant child with them. Surely the rule was not intended to be applied in such cases.

Example: The converse form of this fallacy might be shown by an argument that attempts to refute the principle that lying is wrong by pointing out that a counselor would be justified in lying to keep from betraying a confidence. This example shows that the unusual circumstances that constitute a legitimate exception to a principle sometimes involve another principle that is regarded as having greater worth or priority.

Attacking the Fallacy: One way of pointing out the fallacious character of a particular misapplication of a generalization is to analyze very carefully what the purpose of the particular rule or principle is and then to show that, in the case in question, the purpose of the principle is not being fulfilled or is superseded by some more important, conflicting principle. An attempt should be made, however, to show that the unusual case in question really is an exception by virtue of its special circumstances rather than simply a counterexample to the claim.

Fallacy of the Golden Mean

Definition: This fallacy consists in assuming that the mean or middle view between two extremes must be the best or right one simply because it is the middle view.

Another name for this bit of faulty thinking is the fallacy of moderation. It is assumed—indeed it is a part of our conventional wisdom—that a moderate position is always the best simply because it is moderate. In many situations, a moderate view may in fact be the best or most justifiable position to take; but it is

[4]See Chapter IX, pp. 109–112.

not the best simply because it is a moderate position. In some cases it is the so-called extreme or radical solution to a problem that is the most defensible one. Hence, it could be said that the fact that a particular position is a moderate one is irrelevant to its worth.

Although a compromise is sometimes *necessary* to settle a dispute or resolve a conflict, it cannot be assumed that a compromise solution is always the *best* one. It might well be the case that the position of one of the parties involved in the dispute or conflict has no legitimacy whatsoever. Therefore, though it could be said that it is *not* a fallacy to compromise in order to settle a dispute, it *is* a fallacy to assume, apart from evidence, that a compromise solution is the best one.

Example: Prior to former President Nixon's resignation, several people suggested that we should simply censure Mr. Nixon, as that would avoid the extremes of removal through impeachment and acquittal. There may have been good reasons for censuring the former President, but one of those reasons should not have been that it was the middle course.

Example: Consider the following argument that is sometimes put forth regarding the Israeli-Arab conflict: "Both the Arab and Israeli points of view represent extremes. Therefore, some kind of compromise must be the best solution." Compromise may be the only way that the dispute can be finally settled, but it is a different thing to say that a compromise per se is the best solution in that conflict.

Example: Suppose you are looking for a used refrigerator for your apartment and you find one that you like at a used furniture store. The seller wants 100 dollars for it, and you offer 70 dollars. Because the two of you are far apart on the price, you suggest "splitting the difference" at 85 dollars. Although such a compromise may seem fair to you, it may not be the best solution to the problem. On the one hand, it is possible that the seller already has 85 dollars invested in it and needs to make some profit. On the other hand, it is possible that it may not be worth 85 dollars in the used furniture market. Indeed, your original offer may have been a very fair one.

Attacking the Fallacy: If an arguer proposes a moderate position with regard to an issue, insist that he or she justify the worth of that position. It could also be helpful to keep in mind that there may be two contexts of "best" in any particular situation. A compromise may be the "best" way to resolve a difficult situation; for example, it may prevent continued economic deprivation, bloodshed, or mental anguish. However, it may not be the "best" in the sense of being the most accurate, justifiable, or morally responsible solution to the problem. Nevertheless, you may have to accept the compromise without granting that it is the most justifiable solution. In order to maintain your logical integrity and protect yourself against charges of inconsistency or betrayal in the future, it might be wise to make it clear which of the "bests" you are accepting. Finally, if your attack upon the fallacy of the golden mean fails to convince the arguer that his or her thinking is fallacious, try an absurd example. Ask if the best way to behave in the voting booth would be to "compromise" and vote for exactly one-half the Republicans and one-half the Democrats.

Faulty Analogy

Definition: This fallacy consists in assuming that because two things are alike in one or more respects, they necessarily are alike in some other respect.

Those who commit this fallacy overlook the possibility of significant differences in compared cases and therefore draw a questionable conclusion from a comparison. Commonly two compared things are alike only in unimportant ways and are quite different in important ways, that is, in ways that are relevant to the issue at stake in the argument. But even if the analogy is not faulty in this way, it is not likely that it could lead to an entirely satisfactory conclusion. Analogical arguments are usually only suggestive, and because of this feature of the analogical argument itself, it is frequently difficult to assess precisely how or where it may be weak or defective. Hence, those who present an argument from analogy should be prepared to offer evidence in addition to pointing out any observed similarities. If a claim is made that a conclusion can be drawn about the one from the other, then there should be evidence presented to show precisely *how* the compared cases are alike in the significant way that is relevant to the claim at issue. An observed similarity, by itself, does not constitute evidence.

Example: Suppose someone defended open textbook examinations with the following argument: "No one objects to the practice of a physician looking up a difficult case in medical books. Why, then, shouldn't students taking a difficult examination be permitted to use their textbooks?" With very little reflection, it will be clear that there is little similarity between the compared cases at all. The only thing that seems at all similar is the act of looking inside a book for some assistance in solving a problem. But there the alleged similarity stops. Very different purposes are served by such an act in the two situations. One is specifically designed to test a person's knowledge; the other functions as a means of helping the doctor to diagnose a patient's problem. The doctor's basic knowledge has already been tested by virtue of his or her status as a licensed physician. In order for this analogical argument to be nonfallacious, the arguer would have to present evidence to demonstrate that the two functions do not significantly differ.

Example: "Smoking cigarettes is just like ingesting arsenic into your system. Both have been shown to be causally related to death. So if you wouldn't want to take a spoonful of arsenic, I would think that you wouldn't want to continue smoking." Though it is true that both the ingestion of arsenic and the smoking of cigarettes have been shown to be causally related to human death, there are some significant differences in the character of those causal relations. A single heavy dose of arsenic poisoning will bring about immediate death, whereas the heavy smoking of cigarettes would be likely to bring about premature death only as a result of a long process of deterioration or disease. In one case, then, death is immediate and certain; in the other, death is statistically neither immediate nor certain. Thus, the analogy is faulty.

Example: "If one were to listen to only one kind of music or eat only one kind of food, it would soon become tasteless or boring. Variety makes eating and listening exciting and enriching experiences. Therefore, it could be concluded that an exclusive sexual relationship with only one member of the opposite sex for the rest of one's life—that is, marriage—does not hold out much hope for very much excitement or enrichment." Though such an argument might have some initial force, in order for it to be a strong argument, the arguer would have to demonstrate that an exclusive sexual relationship is not essentially different from an unchanging food diet or an unchanging musical diet. Because human relationships are so complex and so full of a variety of possibilities, it seems likely that a successful counter to such a claim could be produced. However, the burden of proof is on the person who wishes to extend the disadvantages of narrow diets of food and music to exclusive sexual relationships.

Attacking the Fallacy: One of the most effective ways of blunting the force of an argument from analogy is to formulate a counteranalogy, which allows you to draw a conclusion that contradicts that of the arguer. Such a device would demonstrate at least the inconclusiveness of an argument from analogy. However, if you are using a counteranalogy to make a serious claim, make sure that you can provide convincing evidence that the compared cases are similar in an important or significant sense. If you are not able to come up with a counteranalogy or if you are not concerned to make a counterclaim, all you may be able to do, when confronted with a weak or faulty analogy, is to point out that the two compared cases resemble each other only in unimportant or irrelevant ways. Therefore, no inference should be drawn concerning the claim at issue. In no case, of course, should you allow a clever analogy monger to think that simply pointing out interesting similarities qualifies as evidence for any claim.

Fallacy of Novelty

Definition: This fallacy consists in assuming and arguing that a new idea, law, policy, or action is good simply because it is new.

There is nothing inherently worthwhile about something novel simply because it is novel. Every idea, law, policy, or action requires a defense independent of its novel character. A pattern of reasoning that assumes that whatever is novel is better would result in an absurd situation in which *every* proposed alternative to the present way of doing things would demand one's acceptance. Nevertheless, such reasoning is not uncommon, although it usually takes a more subtle form. For example, many of us at one time or another have thought that the problems in our church would be solved if we got a new minister, or that our country's problems would be solved when a different administration with fresh ideas took over in Washington.

Example: A sign in front of a restaurant or service station with the words "Under New Management" is usually intended to convey to the passer-by that the food or service will be better than in the past. However, no reason is usually given for believing such a claim. If we patronize such a place in the expectation of better food or service, we have committed the fallacy of novelty no less than the person who erected the sign.

Example: Consider this argument presented by Dean Henderson to an unconvinced faculty: "We *have* to institute this new curriculum if we are going to meet the challenge of the future. . . . I just don't understand why you are dragging your feet against our attempts to improve our programs here." The Dean has presented no argument for the superiority of his curriculum except that it is new. The Dean simply assumes that the novelty of the curriculum is sufficient reason for its adoption. Yet it would be ironic, indeed, if a member of the academic community, whose very function is to instruct in the art of careful inquiry, would vote to accept a curriculum simply on the basis of its newness.

Attacking the Fallacy: Attacking the fallacy of novelty is not an easy task, for the advertising industry has acculturated all of us to the idea that "new" is tantamount to "improved" or "better." Indeed, it is common sense to believe that energy is expended in developing new products, legislation, or ideas primarily because of the desire to make them better. It is not unreasonable to believe that most new things *are* better in some way. However, the fact that most new things may be better should not lead to the conclusion that *every* new thing is better. The problem, then, becomes convincing those who commit this fallacy that they should not assume that any *particular* product or idea is better simply because of its newness. One way of doing this might be to confront your opponent with some new idea or product he or she would obviously find absurd or at least not better. This demonstration might raise serious questions about the soundness of the "new is better" assumption and encourage your opponent to eliminate novelty as a consideration in an evaluation of worth.

Exercises

A. Identify the type of unwarranted assumption in each of the following:

1. People who have to have a cup of coffee every morning before they can function have no less a problem than alcoholics who have to have their alcohol each day to sustain them.

2. If a doctor is justified in deceiving a sick person, and if there is nothing wrong with telling children about Santa Claus, then we must reject the view that "lying is wrong."

3. A: No, thank you. I don't care for any decaffeinated coffee. It just doesn't taste right.

B: But this is better. It's a completely new way of preparing it.

4. I don't see why you have criticized this novel as implausible. There isn't a single incident in it that couldn't have happened.

5. Anyone who eats meat tacitly condones the killing of animals. We might just as well condone the killing of human beings, for how do we draw the line between one form of animal life and another?

6. Harvard University is one of the best universities in this country, so it must have an outstanding philosophy department. Why don't you apply to do graduate work there?

7. The way I see it is that we must either spend enough money on our football program to make us competitive with some of the better teams in this region or simply drop the program altogether.

8. A: Give me some time to think about it. I want to consider very carefully whether to have sexual relations with you. In other words, I want to try to make a rational decision about it.

   B: Look, darling! Having sex with someone is *not* something you usually make a rational decision about.

9. God must exist; otherwise, life would be unbearable.

10. Look, if you're going to smoke, you're going to take in tar and nicotine. That's clear. Even if *your* cigarette has very little tar and nicotine, the *issue* is that you're taking that stuff into your body—and it has been proven that tar and nicotine kill. Smoking is smoking; that's all there is to it.

B. From among all the fallacies studied to this point, choose the fallacy that most closely resembles the problem exhibited in each of the following:

11. Some students want our college dorms to be completely "open" to members of the opposite sex, 24 hours a day. Others want a "closed" dorm policy—that is, one that makes the dorms off limits to any member of the opposite sex, anytime. Wouldn't the best solution be to have the dorms open about 12 hours in a day, perhaps from noon to midnight?

12. Each of the members of the Board of Trustees has demonstrated superior judgment and skill in handling his or her personal affairs. Therefore, I think we can be assured that the Board will exercise superior judgment and skill in handling the affairs of this institution.

13. Because the Democratic Party supports a program of national health insurance, I assume that Congressman Foster, who is a member of the Democratic Party, will support such a program.

14. Because *human* bodies become less active as they grow older, and because they eventually die, it is reasonable to expect that *political* bodies will become less and less active the longer they are in existence, and that they too will eventually die.

15. Farmer to son: "Son, if you pick up that newborn calf over there *once* every day, your muscles should develop to the point that you would be able to lift it when it is a full-grown cow. The calf will gain just a tiny bit of weight each day; and that little bit of weight can't make any significant difference in your ability to lift it. If you can do it one day, you should be able to do it the next day."

16. You're not going to vote for a man who would give an interview to a magazine like *Playboy*, are you?

17. Did you vote for him for President because he is a Democrat or because he promised to reorganize and simplify the federal bureaucracy?

18. I think that capital punishment for murderers and rapists is quite justified; there are a number of good reasons for putting to death people who commit such crimes.

19. A: No . . . I don't think that I'll join your group. I'm really
not a very religious person.

B: Really? I never knew that you didn't believe in God.

20. Young gymnast to another: "I think our gymnastic show tomorrow will be a very good one, since this is the only time that our parents will be able to see us perform and obviously we want to do a really good job for them."

IV
Fallacies of Missing Evidence

The fallacies discussed in this chapter are ways of reasoning that use no evidence at all or only the appearance of evidence. Though it is true that nearly all fallacious arguments are lacking in proper evidential support, the essential character of these fallacies is the sheer absence of relevant evidence.

Fallacy of Negative Proof

Definition: This fallacy consists in assuming that a claim is true because it is not proved false, or false because it is not proved true. Moreover, it assumes that a claim is true because of the inability or the refusal of an arguer to present convincing evidence *against* it, or that a claim is false because of the inability or the refusal of an arguer to present convincing evidence *for* it.

What makes this kind of argument fallacious is that it uses the lack of evidence for one claim as positive evidence for an opposing claim. In such arguments, the alleged "evidence" for the opposing claim is actually no evidence at all. The conclusion is thereby supported by one's ignorance rather than one's knowledge. For this reason, this fallacy is sometimes referred to as the fallacy of appeal to ignorance. If p is unproved, one cannot legitimately infer that *not p* is proved. The most that one can infer, apart from other evidence, is that *not p* is also unproved. Absence of proof for one claim does not constitute proof for any other claim.

The pattern of reasoning in this fallacy violates a standard methodological principle that the burden of proof for *any* claim generally rests upon the person who sets forth the claim. When one commits the fallacy in question, one is attempting to shift the obligation of proof to another person, usually to someone who is unconvinced by or skeptical about the claim. This is usually done by insisting that the critic *disprove* the claim or provide support for the contradictory claim, rather than assuming one's own obligation to provide support for the original proposal.

There are, however, some situations of inquiry in which this kind of reasoning seems to be acceptable. In our judicial procedure, for example, a defendant is assumed to be innocent unless proven guilty. It should be noted, however, that *innocent* in this context is a highly technical term, which actually means *not proven guilty*. Moreover, when a jury pronounces a verdict of *not guilty*, it is not thereby claimed that the defendant did not commit the act as charged; it is only claimed that the evidence is not weighty enough to prove such a charge. In a judicial proceeding, for practical reasons some decision must be made. Hence, it has been determined that, for legal purposes, a person should be regarded "as if" he or she were innocent unless there is convincing evidence to the contrary.

Another situation in which common sense seems to support reasoning that resembles the fallacy of negative proof is when a thorough search has failed to produce evidence for a particular claim. In such a case, there is a tendency to allow the lack of evidence for a claim to count as evidence against it or *for* its contradictory. For example, it does seem like common sense to assume that, if there is no evidence to support the claim that there *are* termites in your house, it would be justifiable to conclude that there are *no* termites in your house. The point here is that there are a few situations in which it is possible to make a reasonably thorough examination of all evidence relevant to a claim and to discover that no evidence supports the positive thesis. In such cases it seems justifiable to infer the negative thesis. In contrast, the claim that there are extraterrestrial creatures is one for which it is *not* possible to make a reasonably thorough examination of all relevant evidence; so it would not be justifiable to infer anything about the *non*existence of extraterrestrial life.

We must be very cautious about assuming anything on the basis of the lack of evidence concerning an opposing claim. Perhaps such an inference would be warranted only in a case in which it is possible to examine all relevant evidence for the claim. The safest course, however, might be simply to act "as if" the common sense inference were true, if a thorough search produced no convincing evidence to support its contradictory; for if we make the outright assertion that the claim in question is true, we must then take on the burden of proof, a task for which we might not be presently equipped.

Example:

A: Did you get that teaching job at the University of Virginia?
B: No. I sent in my application over two months ago, and I never heard a word from them.

The applicant is assuming that he has been rejected by the university, even though the only "evidence" for a rejection is that there is no evidence for any other claim regarding the status of his application. However, it would be inappropriate to conclude that he had been rejected for the teaching job on the basis of no communication from the university, especially as the institutional procedure required for filling a teaching position is usually a very long and involved one.

Example: "Unless you can produce evidence that former President Nixon did not orchestrate all the Watergate crimes, I am going to assume that he did." The speaker in this case has attempted to shift the burden of proof to the opponent. That person may be skeptical of the speaker's claim yet unwilling or uninterested in supporting the opposing claim. Moreover, the transferred burden of proof requires proving a negative claim: that is, proving that something is not the case, which is usually quite difficult.

Example: Because archaeologists have never found any evidence that Atlantis existed, it might be concluded that the stories about such a city, though intriguing, are simply false. The lack of evidence for ancient Atlantis tends to lead one to the conclusion that no such city ever existed. However, it would be safer to remain skeptical, because of that lack of evidence, but to refrain from making a negative claim.

Example: "What's all this business about equal pay for women? The women who work in my office must be satisfied with their salaries, because not one of them has ever complained or asked for a raise." The speaker is assuming that the situation of a group of people must be satisfactory, simply because no complaints about that situation have been expressed. In other words, the absence of evidence *against* the satisfactory character of a situation is regarded as evidence *for* the satisfactory character of that situation. Making such an inference is so distinctive a form of the fallacy of negative proof that it is often given a separate name—the fallacy of quietism. But from the fact that a person or group is "quiet"—that is, makes no complaints—one could in no way infer that there is nothing to complain about. There may indeed be many good reasons the complaints are not openly voiced.

Attacking the Fallacy: If the absence of proof against a claim could be regarded as proof for it, then even the most bizarre of claims could allegedly be proved. If your verbal opponent makes what you consider a highly questionable claim and supports it by pointing out the lack of evidence against it, it might be well to make what you think he or she would consider an equally questionable claim and support it by the same method.

You could also show how one could be led to logically contradictory conclusions if the pattern of thinking in question were not fallacious. Suppose someone suggests that because psychokinesis has not been proved false, it must be true. Some other person could argue that because psychokinesis has not been proved true, it must be false. Such reasoning would lead us to the conclusion that psychokinesis has been both proved and disproved.

Finally, it might be helpful to distinguish carefully between asserting that "I have no reason to believe that X is true" and asserting that "X is false." The first does not entail the second. Each is a distinct claim. The first explains why one is not now prepared to make a judgment about X; the second is a claim about X that requires evidential support.

Contrary-to-Fact Hypothesis

Definition: This fallacy consists in making a poorly supported claim about what might have happened in the past if other conditions had been present, or about an event that might occur in the future. The fallacy also consists in treating hypothetical claims as if they were statements of fact.

Because *empirical* evidence for claims about nonexistent events is obviously not available, any alleged "evidence" must be regarded as part of an imaginative construct. Though there is usually no way of knowing what might have been or what may be the consequences of an unfulfilled hypothetical event, there may be good reasons or other evidence for a well-supported hypothetical construct about it. Such constructs might be helpful in understanding the past and in planning for, or avoiding undesirable consequences in, the future. However, it must be remembered that such constructs are speculative and thus quite uncertain. They are at best "likely stories." The question arises, then, as to whether there is any fallaciousness in constructing an imaginative hypothesis. It is my judgment that making a claim about an unfulfilled hypothetical event is fallacious only insofar as it is not well supported or its speculative character is not acknowledged. The contrary-to-fact hypothesis is fallacious, then, if it is a *weak* hypothesis or if it is treated as a statement of actual fact.

Example: Consider the following contrary-to-fact hypotheses, none of which is provided with any support: "If you had only tasted the stewed snails, you would have loved them." "If you had studied a little harder, you would have passed the exam." "If only I had practiced a little more on my backhand, I could have won that tennis tournament." Such claims are usually totally lacking in support and therefore rarely merit acceptance.[1] There may indeed be good reasons to accept such constructs, but the arguer has not provided us with any of those reasons.

Example: "If I hadn't goofed around my first year in college, I would have been accepted at medical school." Again, though it may be possible to make a good case for this speculative claim, no such case is actually presented.

Example: Consider the number of students who have convinced themselves or their parents, with something like the following "argument," of the wisdom of moving out of campus housing: "If I could just live off campus, I could get a lot more studying done, my grades would improve, and I'm sure I would get a lot more sleep." No doubt the student thinks that there are good reasons to support these claims; yet listeners are expected to accept such claims without hearing those reasons.

[1]It is possible, of course, that the context of a claim will provide some support for it.

Attacking the Fallacy: Because the formulation of imaginative constructs is a vital part of planning for the future and understanding the past, in no way would I encourage anyone to pounce upon every hypothetical construct or to refrain from exercising one's own imagination. However, if you are confronted with a substantive contrary-to-fact claim that is highly questionable, I would suggest that you find some way of getting your opponent to recognize and to admit to the speculative character of the claim. Sometimes the very act of admitting that a claim is speculative will lead one to be more open to counterarguments and to take more seriously the task of supporting it. The fact that one may clearly admit the speculative nature of a claim does not relieve one of the obligation to provide good reasons in support of it.

One effective way of confronting an unsupported hypothetical claim might be to inform your opponent that you are in no position to respond to the claim in the absence of evidence. You might say, "Well, you may be right, but I would have no way of determining that, as I am not aware of your evidence for such a claim." Your opponent will probably feel obligated to make some attempt to provide you with evidence, and that should at least get the discussion on a constructive track.

Unsuitable Use of a Cliché

Definition: This fallacy consists in using an aphorism or cliché in place of relevant evidence for a claim.

The fallacy commonly takes the form of using a cliché or aphorism to express an argument or opinion and failing to show that the proposition expressed by it is reliable. Indeed, the fact that many clichés or aphorisms seem to contradict each other suggests that depending upon a cliché for one's insight or direction is highly questionable. Do not the following sets of aphorisms seem to give contradictory advice? (1) "Two heads are better than one" and "Too many cooks spoil the broth." (2) "Where there's smoke there's fire" and "You can't tell a book by its cover." (3) "He who hesitates is lost" and "Fools rush in where angels fear to tread." (4) "Better safe than sorry" and "Nothing ventured, nothing gained." (5) "A new broom sweeps clean" and "Many a good tune is played on an old fiddle." (6) "Where there's a will, there's a way" and "If wishes were horses, beggars would ride."

Aphorisms or clichés are not really arguments at all; they are simply expressions of popular wisdom, and the "wisdom" expressed in many aphorisms can easily be contradicted by the "wisdom" expressed in others. Hence, apart from other evidence, there is no reason to regard an aphorism as reliable support for any claim or course of action.

Example: Suppose that a marriage counselor says to a young woman that she can't be married and relate sexually to another man at the same time. In an attempt to convince her, he says, "You just can't have your cake and eat it too." Such an aphorism is inapplicable in this particular instance. Having or keeping a piece of cake and consuming that same cake are logically incompatible, but there is nothing logically incompatible about being married, and remaining so, and also relating sexually to another person.

Example: A typical campus cliché expressed by one student to another the night before an important test is: "Well, if you don't know it now, you never will." No evidence is usually given for such a questionable claim; indeed, there is considerable evidence to suggest that it is a false claim. As far as performance on tests is concerned, it is probably safe to say that a conscientious student might learn a significant amount of material during the hours immediately before a test.

Example: Sometimes a cliché is simply used as a substitute for good reasons or an appropriate response. Suppose that a parent, before leaving for the day, gives very clear instructions to a child to cut the grass. Upon returning, the parent finds that the grass cutting is only half finished. When the child is asked why the job is not completed, his or her response is: "Rome wasn't built in a day." It is true that 24 hours isn't enough time to build a city the size of Rome, but 8 to 10 hours does provide enough time to cut an average-sized yard. In this case, the familiar proverb is an inappropriate or meaningless response to a legitimate question.

Attacking the Fallacy: Because clichés, like analogies, are at best only suggestive, it is my advice that no argument wholly constituted by a cliché be treated as a serious one. If the cliché were accompanied by a thoroughly developed argument that demonstrated why the cliché or aphorism expressed an important and defensible insight, the cliché itself would add nothing to the argument; it would only be a clever way of expressing the argument's conclusion. In no way should you be intimidated by the allegedly obvious wisdom of a popular cliché. A cliché or aphorism, like any other not so cleverly expressed opinion, requires evidential support or good reasons to make it worthy of acceptance. If an arguer in any way attempts to let an argument rest on a cliché, challenge it directly; or better yet, counter it, if possible, with a cliché that gives contradictory advice. The arguer would then have to show why the original cliché is better founded than yours.

Inference from a Label

Definition: This fallacy consists in assuming that evaluative or identifying words or phrases attached to people or things constitute a sufficient reason for drawing conclusions about the objects to which such labels are attached.

This is a fallacy many advertisers expect the typical consumer to commit; thus they advertise in a way that lends itself to such faulty inference. The manufacturer of Super-flite Golf Balls would like weekend golfers to infer, from nothing more than the name, that using such balls will lengthen their drive. The discount houses would like consumers to infer, simply from the fact that they are called "discount" houses, that name-brand goods may be purchased there for lower prices. The manufacturers of an auto wax would like possible users of their product to assume that the wax is simple to apply just because they have what they call an "easy applicator." And who has not been tempted to stop for coffee when the sign reads: "The World's Best Cup of Coffee"? Yet in each case, absolutely no evidence is given to support the claim in question. While evaluative or descriptive labels or names may whet our appetite or increase our interest in investigating particular claims, it would be foolish to assume anything, without further inquiry, about the objects to which such labels are attached.

Example: Probably we have all had the experience of being tired and hungry after driving a long time on an automobile trip and have found ourselves mildly elated when a sign tells us that there are "delicious food" and "clean restrooms" ahead. However, in some cases the only valuable thing about the stop was that it gave us one more opportunity to learn about the importance of not inferring anything from signs.

Example: "Emory & Henry College must be a good school, for the college catalog says that it is a fine liberal arts college of the highest caliber." Emory & Henry may indeed be a fine school, but that could not be legitimately inferred solely from the description in its catalog.

Example: "What do you mean by saying that the Democratic Party doesn't express the will of the people? The very name of the party means that everyone has a voice in what is done." There is no more reason to believe, on the basis of a name, that the Democratic Party is democratic than to infer, for the same reason, that the Justice Department is just.

Attacking the Fallacy: In spite of what has been said about the folly of inferring anything from signs or labels, you need not be skeptical about evaluatively neutral signs such as "You are now entering Yellowstone National Park." There does not seem to be any good reason to question whether or not you are actually entering Yellowstone Park. However, if a sign in any way includes an evaluation or a description with evaluative overtones, then there is good reason to be skeptical about that part of the claim. For example, if you see a sign at the service station indicating that it has clean restrooms, there is no good reason to doubt that the service station has restrooms; but there is no reason to infer, from the sign, that they are clean. I am suggesting that you avoid becoming a sign-skeptic yet not fall victim to the schemes, prejudices, or ignorance of the advertiser. In other words, hold your response to evaluative descriptions until you have something more than a label on which to base your conclusion.

Neglect of Relevant Evidence

Definition: This fallacy consists in arguing in a way that ignores, suppresses, or unfairly minimizes the importance of obvious evidence unfavorable to one's position.

If one holds very strongly to some particular point of view or conclusion, it is tempting to neglect or suppress evidence that could possibly throw that judgment into question. A subtle form of this fallacy is to regard counterevidence as less relevant than it really is or to give it less weight than it deserves. Indeed, the conviction may be so strong that one is not even aware of improperly evaluating counterevidence to the claim. This pattern of reasoning violates a standard methodological principle of inquiry that one is obligated to investigate all sides of an issue and to accept the position that is best supported by the evidence.

It should perhaps be pointed out that there are at least two instances in our culture where deliberate "slanting" or neglecting of evidence seems to be acceptable. One is in our adversary method of judicial procedure. The arguments of both the defense and the prosecution are presented with a very deliberate neglect of counterevidence. However, it is *not* acceptable for the jury and the judge to neglect any evidence in coming to a fair judgment in a particular case. The other situation in which slanting, unfortunately, seems to be acceptable is in debating clubs and tournaments on the high school and college level.[2] In this context the issue is not primarily arriving at the best answer to the question on which the debate is focused; it is evaluating the relative forensic abilities of the opposing debaters. However, winning a court case or winning a debate tournament is not the principal concern of one who is interested in the truth. Indeed, we should welcome the presentation of any evidence that might point out weaknesses in our position. If that evidence can be shown not to be damaging in any way, we can be all the more assured of the truth of our position. On the other hand, if that counterevidence is significantly damaging to our position, we should be grateful; it may lead us closer to the truth by steering us away from an indefensible or highly questionable conclusion.

Example: The following argument concerning the busing of school children to achieve racial desegregation is not infrequently heard. "Some children have to spend several hours a day traveling to and from school; they are separated from their neighborhood friends; they cannot participate easily in after-school or pre-school extracurricular activities; and the taxpayers have to pay for the added expense of buses, drivers, and gasoline. It seems obvious from these facts that we ought to stop this insanity immediately." The arguer has apparently neglected to consider the moral desirability of the goal busing is designed to achieve and the possibility that such a goal may not be achievable by any other method.

Example: "Motorcycles are dangerous; they are noisy; only two people can ride at once; you can't ride them in cold or rainy weather; in most states you are required to wear an uncomfortable helmet; and the grease from the motor can completely ruin your clothes. I can't see why anyone would want to buy one." The arguer has neglected to consider many other factors relevant to the desirability of owning a motorcycle. For example, the motorcycle is a relatively inexpensive form of transportation; it is more maneuverable than a car; it is easier to find a place to park it; and many people simply find it more enjoyable than a car.

Example: "I can't see why anyone would want to go to the movies rather than watch television. After all, with television you can sit in the privacy of your

[2]It should be noted, however, that in both judicial and debate procedures, the *opposition* is specifically charged with the responsibility of presenting contrary evidence.

own home; you don't have to pay for the movies you see; you don't have to get dressed up; and you don't have to pay those exorbitant prices for candy and drinks. Also, you don't have to fight the traffic or pay for gasoline and parking the car." This kind of argument could possibly persuade a number of people to stay home and watch television; but for many others it neglects a number of important factors. Television does not usually run movies until they are two or three years old; many people find it very enjoyable to dress up and go out for an evening; and many of the films that are shown at theaters probably never will be shown on television. These factors ought at least to be considered when one is evaluating the relative merits of watching television and going to film theaters.

Attacking the Fallacy: Do not be surprised if one who presents you with an argument fails to accompany it with all the evidence against its conclusion. It is quite possible, of course, to assume that the arguer has considered such evidence and is of the opinion that it constitutes no real danger to the claim at issue and therefore deserves no mention. However, in view of our general tendency to neglect evidence damaging to our favorite opinions, such an assumption would probably not be warranted. Hence, it seems to me that it is legitimate to ask an arguer to give at least some indication that all relevant factors have been seriously evaluated.

No one of us wants to lose an argument, mainly because we think we are correct in what we are saying. However, I would not want to win an argument by "cheating," that is, by deliberately neglecting evidence that I knew was damaging to my case, just as I would not want to win a tennis game by cheating, for example, by calling a close, but "in," ball "out." It is quite possible that I might think that I am really a better player than my opponent, but I could hardly justify my cheating to prove it; for in tennis, the best player is determined as the one who wins the game. In reasoning, the best judgment is the one that is best supported in view of *all* the evidence. I could not feel comfortable claiming that my opinion was correct if I could "prove" my case only by neglecting important evidence. If your opponent has neglected important evidence, it would probably not be discreet to accuse him or her of cheating. But surely there is nothing inappropriate about calling that evidence to his or her attention. If the arguer refuses to consider such evidence, then you could only conclude that he or she is not really interested in the truth or in following standard procedures of inquiry.

Exercises

A. Identify the type of fallacy of missing evidence in each of the following:

1. If Gerald Ford had been elected in 1976, we wouldn't be in the economic mess we are in today.

2. The son of former Teamster President Jimmy Hoffa, speaking of his father's disappearance: "I believe it's an abduction. There's no evidence it isn't. We have no reason to believe it isn't. . . . The key question is who? We just don't know who did it."

3. How can you say that this cereal doesn't have any nutritional value? Just look at the box. See, it says: "Good tasting and good for you, too!"

4. **Daughter:** But, mother, I have given you several good reasons why you should let me go to Susan's party. Why won't you let me go?

   Mother: Just remember, dear, that "mother knows best."

5. I don't see any reasons for attending classes. They are time consuming. There are many things that I would much rather do. I can use the time I save not going to class to do more reading and preparation for the tests. Besides, if I go to class I have to take a shower, get dressed, walk to class in the cold, and, when I get there, sit in an uncomfortable chair for an hour forcing myself to laugh at the stupid jokes of the professors.

6. If I just hadn't dropped out of college, I'd be working now rather than standing in this unemployment line.

7. It's my advice to you to quit college and take this job right now. This is too good an opportunity to pass up. Remember: "It's the early bird that gets the worm."

8. The black people in this country must be happy with their situation now. There haven't been any protest marches or any loud voices of dissent for several years.

9. Why would anyone want to climb Mt. Everest? The slope is steep, treacherous, and barren, the temperature is unbelievably cold; and one takes considerable risk to one's life. Besides, what can you do after you get to the top—just turn around and come back down. The whole thing seems worthless to me.

10. **A:** I'll never learn to read; I'm just plain stupid.

    B. You're wrong, Abel; you *can* learn.

    A. No, I can't. Haven't you heard what all the kids call me? "Dumb Abel!" That's what they call me. So you see? I'll never learn to read.

B. From among all the fallacies studied to this point, choose the fallacy that most closely resembles the problem exhibited in each of the following:

11. I'm sorry, Mr. Dunbar, but we cannot approve your loan application. We must assume that your credit is no good, because there is no record indicating that you have ever met any monthly installment payments.

12. If I had gone with him to the party, I could have kept him from making a fool of himself.

13. **A:** The Surgeon General's report on smoking and health says that the death rate for smokers of cigarettes is about 70 percent higher than that for nonsmokers.

    B: Really? That is the most impressive argument for immortality that I have heard yet.

14. The Constitution grants me the right of free speech, so there is no way you can stop me from talking anywhere I please. What makes you think that you, a college librarian, can deny me my basic right of free speech?

15. I don't see any good reason to stop smoking cigarettes. They help me to relax; I like the taste of them; they give me something to do with my hands; and they keep me from gaining weight, which is probably the best reason of all, because the less I smoke the more I eat.

16. **A:** Have you seen *King Kong*?

    B: I saw the old one. But I didn't really care for it.

    A: You'd like the new one. It surely must be better than the original or they wouldn't have gone to all that trouble to make it.

17. One senatorial candidate says of the opposition candidate: "Ms. Bradford should come before the American people and make a complete financial statement as to her financial history, and if she doesn't, it will be an admission that she has something to hide."

18. Nobody keeps to the 55-mile-an-hour speed limit. Most everybody drives at least 60. The speed limit really ought to be raised at least 5 miles an hour.

19. You could put all of your savings in government bonds or you could invest all of it in the stock market, but it would be best to avoid either extreme by investing half of it in government bonds and the other half in the stock market.

20. **A:** If that were a child of mine, I would have given him a good spanking rather than sitting down and talking with him about his behavior as you did.

    B: Why do you think that your method is better?

    A: I just think that "if you spare the rod, you spoil the child."

V
Causal Fallacies

This chapter discusses faulty reasoning about the causal relationships between events. Trying to understand the notion of *cause* has been an important and difficult philosophical problem for a long time, and this difficulty underlies a number of problems in reasoning. Rather than grouping all of these problems under the label of *false cause,* as some texts do, I have tried to distinguish as carefully as possible the different ways in which logical confusion has been exhibited in reasoning about causal relationships.

Confusion of a Necessary with a
Sufficient Condition

Definition: This fallacy consists in assuming that a necessary condition of an event is also a sufficient one.

A *necessary condition* of an event is a condition, or set of conditions, in the absence of which the event in question *cannot* occur. A *sufficient condition* of an event is a condition, or set of conditions, in the presence of which the event in question *will* occur. A necessary condition of an event, then, must be present in order for that event to occur; but it alone, in most cases, is not sufficient to produce the event. It is not uncommon for people to assume that an event will occur simply because its necessary condition is present; however, such thinking mistakes a necessary condition for a sufficient one.

Example: It is obviously necessary to water a plant in order to make it grow and stay healthy, but it would be fallacious to assume that watering a plant is sufficient condition for the growth and health of the plant. A number of other conditions must be present also. Similarly, one must read a book in order to understand it, but reading it will not guarantee understanding it. Assuming that reading a book will guarantee an understanding of it is confusing a necessary condition with a sufficient one.

Example: "You said that I would have to run the mile in less than six minutes to be on the track team, and *I did*. So why is it that I got cut from the team?" The speaker assumed that meeting the eligibility requirement of being able to run a mile in less than six minutes would be a sufficient condition of being on the track team. Meeting the requirement, however, was only a necessary condition. The sufficient condition for being on the track team would probably include the meeting of many other requirements.

Example: Consider the common situation where a professor tells her students at the first of the term that, in order to pass the course, they will have to come to class regularly, read the daily assignments, participate in class discussion, take all tests and examinations, and submit a research paper. Some students have fulfilled such conditions and then have experienced genuine surprise when they failed to pass the course. Such puzzlement could possibly be eliminated if the students understood the difference between the necessary and the sufficient conditions for passing the course. In the case in question, the professor mentioned the necessary but not the sufficient conditions for passing the course.

Attacking the Fallacy: Many people reason in a way that confuses a necessary condition with a sufficient condition because they do not understand exactly how the two differ. Hence, it might be helpful to clarify that distinction carefully when confronting such confusion. One of the most effective ways of doing this might be to use an example that would make the difference unmistakable. Suppose a young woman were to claim that she would become a great concert pianist because she had been practicing two hours a day for fifteen years. It should be plain that, although practicing the piano regularly is a necessary condition of becoming a concert pianist, surely it alone is not a sufficient one. When that distinction becomes clear, your verbal opponent should recognize the problematic character of his or her own argument, which exhibits the same form as the argument in the example.

Causal Oversimplification

Definition: This fallacy consists in oversimplifying the relevant causal antecedents of an event or series of events.

Causal oversimplification often involves introducing factors insufficient to account for the event in question or overemphasizing the role of one or more of those factors. In causal explanations, it is a common practice to point to a very obvious antecedent of an event and to designate it as the cause. However, a careful analysis of the notion of cause would show that the *cause*, or sufficient condition, of an event in most cases includes a considerable number of antecedents that only *together* are sufficient to bring about the event. To point to only one of those factors in a particular causal explanation would most likely be an oversimplification.

Example: "Children spend an average of five hours per day watching television—time that used to be spent reading. That explains why Scholastic Aptitude Test (SAT) scores are dropping." Even if the facts presented were true, it is unlikely that they are sufficient to account for the lower SAT scores. Increased viewing of television and reduction in the amount of reading may well be *one* of the causal antecedents, but to assign that weighty a role to such an event would seem to oversimplify a causally complex phenomenon.

Example: During the presidential campaign of 1968, and shortly after the American spy ship *Pueblo* was captured by North Korean gunboats in the territorial waters of North Korea, Richard Nixon said: "When a third-rate military power can capture a U.S. military ship on the high seas, it's time for a change in Washington." Mr. Nixon appeared to be explaining that such an event was caused by a Democratic administration. His implicit suggestion was that he, not the Democratic nominee, should be elected and then such things as the *Pueblo* incident would not happen. Nixon's explanation simply did not introduce enough factors to account adequately for the event in question. At best he overemphasized the role of one of those factors.

Example: A radio preacher recently argued in the following way: "Marriage would be greatly helped if husband and wife would read the Scriptures together and pray together every day. No wonder divorce abounds when family worship has dropped over 90 percent, and in some places almost 100 percent." Apart from questions that might be raised about the reliability of the facts regarding the drop in the rate of family worship, it does not seem that the rise in the national divorce rate could be sufficiently accounted for by such data. Because the reasons for the dissolution of a marriage are usually quite varied and complex, it seems inappropriate to reduce them to one principal factor.

Attacking the Fallacy: It is almost always possible to question another's causal explanation, for an explanation of an event rarely includes *all* the literally hundreds of antecedent conditions that constitute the sufficient condition of that event. The question, then, is determining when a person has included enough of those factors to escape the charge of oversimplification. You should not, of course, expect an arguer to name every antecedent condition of an event in question. To do so would be virtually impossible; it would also be an inefficient use of time and energy. However, you should not allow explanations to be unduly partial or arrived at without sufficient reflection. If you suspect that a causal analysis is oversimplified because it does not seem to account adequately for the event or because it overemphasizes the role of one or more particular factors, point out what problems you have with such an explanation or request some further defense for the adequacy of it. Remember that the burden of proof is upon the one offering the explanation. Another possible approach is to suggest additional factors that you think might make the causal explanation more adequate and then ask your opponent for an evaluation of those suggestions.

Post Hoc Fallacy

Definition: This fallacy consists in assuming that a particular event, B, is caused by another event, A, simply because B follows A in time.

Establishing the temporal priority of one event over another is not a sufficient condition for inferring a causal relationship between those events. One cannot assume that *post hoc, ergo propter hoc*—that an event that occurs after another event occurs, therefore, *because* of that other event. A chronological relationship is only one of the indicators of a causal relationship. Other indicators might include a spatial connection or perhaps some history of regularity. If priority alone were sufficient to establish a causal relationship, then virtually any event that preceded another could be assumed to be the cause of it. This kind of thinking contributed to the creation of many of the superstitions in our culture. Something was often considered "bad luck" for no reason other than the fact that it preceded a misfortune. Such thinking mistakes a sheer coincidence for a causal relation.

Example: "I can't help but think that you are the cause of this problem; we never had any problem with the furnace until you moved into the apartment." The manager of the apartment house, on no stated grounds other than the temporal priority of the new tenant's occupancy, has assumed that the tenant's presence has some causal relationship to the furnace's becoming faulty.

Example: "Ever since we quit going to church, business has been getting worse. If we want to keep from going completely bankrupt, we'd better start back to church." Again, the claim is that one event was brought about by another event simply because of the temporal relationship.

Example: "From the time of the Supreme Court decisions granting the accused more rights, the crime rate has steadily increased. It is the Warren Court that brought about our increasing crime problem." It is conceivable that there is some causal relationship between the judicial situation created by the Warren Court decisions and the increased crime rate, but it would have to be established by more evidence than that of the temporal priority of the Warren Court decisions.

Attacking the Fallacy: It is difficult to believe that anybody really concludes that B is caused by A *simply* because B follows A in time. In most cases there are probably additional factors that lie behind the causal claim. For example, in the illustrations above, the manager of the apartment house may have reason to believe that the tenant has tampered with the furnace, the operator of the business may have well-grounded beliefs about divine punishment, and the critic of the Supreme

Court may be able to present a convincing argument showing how the Warren Court decisions have contributed to the increased crime rate; but the claims themselves focus simply on the temporal character of the relationship of events. Insofar as other factors or assumptions are not specified or even mentioned, it is appropriate to point out the *post hoc* character of a claim and to indicate that you will regard such an explanation as adequate only if it is supplemented by convincing substantial evidence.

If a person commits the so-called *post hoc* fallacy, the question might arise as to why it would not be just as appropriate to charge him or her with the fallacy of causal oversimplification. The *post hoc* fallacy, in my judgment, is not a special case of causal oversimplification. Causal oversimplification usually occurs when particular causal antecedents are regarded as constituting the sufficient condition of an event when they are not by themselves adequate to account for that event. In the case of the *post hoc* fallacy, there is no causal factor being oversimplified; indeed, the problem at issue is whether the events in question have any causal relationship at all.

Confusion of Cause and Effect

Definition: This fallacy consists in confusing the cause with the effect of an event or failing to recognize that there may be a reciprocal causal relation between the two events in question.

It is not always necessary or important to eliminate a confusion that might exist between a cause and an effect. For example, when the Straw Man asks the Wizard of Oz for a brain, the Wizard answers that he cannot give him a brain but that he can give him a diploma from the University of Kansas. The Wizard has confused the brain with the effect of a brain, but nobody really cares, least of all the Straw Man. In the real world, however, resolving such confusion can be very important, in that it can assist us in coming to an accurate understanding of our experiences and in anticipating the future.

Example: "It's no wonder that Phillip makes such good grades and always does what the teacher asks. He's the teacher's pet." It is more likely the case that Phillip is the teacher's pet because he makes good grades and cooperates with the teacher. Moreover, it is possible that there is a reciprocal causal relation between Phillip's being the teacher's pet and his admirable behavior. The fact that Phillip is the teacher's pet would probably cause him to want to make even better grades and to be even more cooperative in his behavior.

Example: An illustration that needs no comment is borrowed from another logic text: While reading a study of sexual behavior, a young married woman who was working on her master's degree learned that intellectuals generally prefer to have the lights on during sexual intercourse, whereas nonintellectuals generally prefer to have the lights turned off. Because it was near the time for her to take her master's examination, she insisted that she and her husband leave the bedroom lights on, in the hope that it would improve her performance on the examination.[1]

Attacking the Fallacy: Any confusion that obscures the truth should be avoided or challenged. For that reason, even if my small child were to say to me: "Look, Daddy, that tree moving over there is making the wind blow," I would consider it less an occasion for being amused than as an opportunity for giving the child a more accurate understanding of the nature of wind. When the thinking of adults exhibits a confusion of cause and effect, then it is all the more dangerous, because adults are in a better position to have an effect upon the thinking of others. Hence, it is my suggestion that any kind of causal explanation that represents what you believe to be a confusion of cause and effect should be challenged in a way that would be constructive in eliminating the confusion. Possibly you could ask the arguer to entertain an alternative understanding of the causal relation on the basis of additional relevant factors to which you might call attention.

Neglect of a Common Cause

Definition: This fallacy consists in failing to recognize that two seemingly related events may not be causally related at all but rather effects of a common cause.

When two events are found together in what appears to be a causal relation, we tend to assume that one is the cause and one the effect. Such thinking, however, can obscure a proper understanding of the relationship. One should always be open to the possibility that both events may be effects of another event, which may not be immediately present. In many cases, however, to discover such a common cause may require one to call upon a backlog of general knowledge. In other words, one might have to draw upon information not provided in the situation.

Example: If it were discovered that most elementary school teachers have children of their own, it might be concluded either that teaching stimulates an interest in parenthood or that being a parent stimulates increased interest in working with children. However, a more likely analysis of that situation is that another factor, the love of children, has caused many people to become both parents and elementary school teachers.

Example: Suppose that a young college student were both obese and depressed. A hasty, but typical, analysis of that situation might very well be that the obesity is causing the depression or that, because of the depression, the student tends to overeat. However, a more likely understanding of this case is that there is some underlying psychological or physical problem that is causing both effects.

[1]Wesley C. Salmon, *Logic* (Englewood Cliffs, N.J.: Prentice-Hall, 1963), p. 76.

Example: It is not infrequently heard that current movies and television are bringing about a "moral degeneration" in our country. In actuality, however, it is probably the case that there are a number of other factors at work in our culture that together are producing both the contemporary trend in films and our changing moral standards. Because these factors are obviously more difficult to detect or to isolate in a causal analysis, it is simpler, although simplistic, to blame the movie makers or the television programmers.

Attacking the Fallacy: Great care should be taken not to falsely charge a person with neglect of a common cause. In almost any causal relationship there will be peripheral factors common to the events in question, the neglect of which would constitute no fallacy. In other words, if one's explanation of the allegedly causal relation between being a school teacher and being a parent failed to mention that being an adult was causally necessary to both effects, it would not be appropriate to charge him or her with neglecting a common cause. The common cause in this case is not a significant or importantly relevant one in the explanation. However, if one is attempting to explain or account for an allegedly causal situation with the two factors at hand, and a more *adequate* account could be provided by appealing to an additional factor causally common to both, then it would indeed be fallacious to neglect that alternative explanation. If you believe that the primary problem with a proposed explanation rests on its neglect of a common cause of the events in question, you should demonstrate just how attention to that feature could provide a more adequate explanation than your opponent's. Your opponent should then feel obligated to scrutinize your proposal: that is, to show, if possible, why it is not a more adequate explanation.

Domino Fallacy

Definition: This fallacy consists in assuming, without appropriate evidence, that a particular action or event is just one, usually the first, in a series of steps that will lead inevitably to some specific consequence.

The name of the domino fallacy derives from the child's game of lining up dominoes on end about an inch apart and then pushing the first one over, causing a chain reaction of falling dominoes. The chain reaction works in the child's game, but not all events are arranged so that a falling-domino effect ensues. For each event in any so-called series of events, an independent argument must be presented, and in no case should one assume that one event will lead to or cause another particular event or series of events without making a separate inquiry into the causal factors involved in each of those allegedly succeeding events.

Example: During the Vietnam War, it was widely argued that "if we let the Communists have Vietnam, they will then take Cambodia, Thailand, then all of Southeast Asia, and before you know it, we will be in a Third World War." However, little evidence was ever presented for the view that there was or would be a causal relation between each of the events in that so-called series of events. Even if one were to try to present such evidence, perhaps by calling attention to the global strategy of the Communist Party, it would still have to be demonstrated that giving up Vietnam was the key or "lead domino" in that strategy.

Example: Examine the following hypothetical argument against allowing students to become members of faculty committees: "If you let students on the Academic Policies Committee, the next thing they will want is to be voting members of departments, and then probably a co-deanship. Before you know it, they will be hiring and firing the faculty." The proposal to put students on certain faculty committees is one for which a number of very good reasons can be given. Whether or not it is wise to elect students as departmental members or to appoint a student as co-Dean requires a separate argument, for presumably different issues would be involved in each case. There is little reason to believe that students would not or could not distinguish between these issues and recognize that one event bears no logical or causal relationship to the other.

Example: Who has not heard arguments similar to the following one by a college professor to his students: "I do not permit questions in my class, because if I allow one student to ask a question, then everyone starts asking questions, and the first thing you know, there is not enough time for my lecture." It seems doubtful that persuasive evidence could be presented to support such a claim. Indeed, a question in the mind of one student is usually independent of any question in the minds of others. At least, no causal relation between them could be justifiably assumed.

Attacking the Fallacy: If you suspect a bit of "domino thinking," insist that the arguer give an independent causal explanation for each event about which a claim is made. Another strategy might be to counter with a claim about some obviously absurd causal series. For example, suggest that if you buy goods on credit, you will soon buy more than you can afford, you won't be able to pay your bills, the finance company will repossess your car, you'll lose your job because you'll have no way to get there, and you'll be so unhappy you will kill yourself—all because you bought a television set on the easy-payment plan. It should be obvious to your opponent that there is no reason to believe that such an event would bring about this series of events. Likewise, it should become obvious that there is little reason to assume any causal relationship between the events in his or her series.

Exercises

A. Identify the type of causal fallacy in each of the following:

1. Former President Gerald Ford lost the election to Jimmy Carter because he agreed to debate him, thereby giving Carter a national exposure that he would not otherwise have had. That's something an incumbent should never do.

2. Senator Foster came out against the strip-mining bill just one week after he had a meeting with the President at the White House. The President must have really applied some pressure.

3. You said that if I'm going to make more friends, I will have to learn to control my temper. Well, I haven't lost my temper in over six months, and as far as I am able to tell, I haven't made a single friend.

4. Son, all it takes is *one* drink to start you on the road to alcoholism. The same is true with marijuana; it's that first smoke that is crucial. If you try it and like it, you'll want more, and the more you smoke, the more dependent you'll become. Then you'll try the harder stuff and finally end up completely "freaked out." Take my word for it; I've seen it happen time and time again.

5. Since the explosion of the first atomic bomb, our weather has been really freakish. That's what happens when humans interfere with nature.

6. Recent studies show that most successful executives have very large vocabularies. I encourage you, then, to develop as large a vocabulary as possible if you wish to have a successful business career.

7. I've noticed that when my dog barks for a long time, it makes him real hungry. Whenever I feed him just after he has been barking for a long time, he really gobbles up his food.

8. Driver to state trooper: "To be within the law, one has to drive 55 miles an hour or less, and I was only driving 50 miles an hour, so there can be no legal reason for you to arrest me!"

9. Medical records show that alcoholics tend to be undernourished. These data strongly suggest that a poor diet contributes to alcoholism.

10. Our study shows that 80 percent of the young people who are heavy users of hard drugs have serious difficulties in relating to their parents. Thus we can conclude that a stricter enforcement of our drug prohibitions could significantly reduce the domestic problems of these young people.

B. From among all the fallacies studied to this point, choose the fallacy that most closely resembles the problem exhibited in each of the following:

11. It is hard for me to see how my neighbors and I can be blamed for discrimination when it comes to deciding who is to live in our neighborhood. We make discriminations all through life. If people are not allowed to discriminate, how can they make decisions in life between right and wrong? Indeed, how can they even act responsibly if they must be indiscriminate in their choices?

12. Because philosophy has never been taught on the high school level before, I see no reason to begin now. If philosophy were suitable for a high school curriculum, it would have been introduced long ago.

13. It was only three months after Harold got married that he started smoking dope. His wife must have got him started on the stuff.

14. David told Dan's friend that he would go with him.

15. I contend that if you speak softly but firmly to your children, they will not be boisterous or undisciplined. That is the way I have brought up my children, and they are, I'm proud to say, very quiet and well-behaved.

16. Because every part of the human body has a particular function, the human organism itself must have some essential or particular function. However, the philosophers and theologians have never been able to agree on what that essential character is.

17. Whether or not they are very good parents, I don't really know, but their kids spend an awful lot of time at the neighbors'—when they're not running around town.

18. The food-stamp program *seems* innocent enough, but once we start providing people with free food, the next thing you know it will be free clothing, then free housing, and eventually probably a guaranteed annual income. Let's stop such madness while we still can. I say that we junk the food-stamp program now.

19. I know that you are not a wealthy man, but I hope that does not embarrass you. There's nothing wrong with being poor.

20. No, I won't discuss my religious beliefs with you. There is nothing that you could say that might make me change my mind.

VI
Fallacies of Irrelevance

The fallacies discussed in this chapter employ premises that are logically irrelevant to their conclusions. Such patterns of reasoning are often called *non sequiturs* or *argumentative leaps*. In a general sense, of course, all fallacious arguments are non sequiturs in that the conclusion does not follow from the premises. Four of the fallacies of irrelevance included in this chapter are *ad hominem* fallacies, so called because they attack or respond to one's opponent personally rather than to his or her argument or point of view. They are fallacies of irrelevance, because the reasons behind such personal attacks are only rarely relevant to the merit of the position.

Missing the Point

Definition: This fallacy consists in drawing a conclusion that "misses the point" of the evidence, although it purports to follow from the evidence; or in presenting evidence that does not support a stated conclusion, although it may support some vaguely similar unstated conclusion.

When this fallacy occurs, the question arises as to whether it should be considered a case of irrelevant evidence or a case of an irrelevant conclusion. If the evidence is not in support of the stated conclusion, we could say that the evidence is irrelevant to that conclusion; but we could also say that the conclusion is irrelevant to the evidence. Whatever we may choose to call it, if there is no relevant relationship between the evidence and the stated conclusion, there is no basis for inferring that conclusion, although there may be a basis for inferring some other, perhaps similar or related, conclusion. In some cases, reasoning in a way that misses the point may be deliberate, as in the case of a prosecutor who is allegedly supporting the claim that the defendant is guilty of rape, yet most all of the "evidence" presented supports another conclusion, namely, that rape is a heinous crime. The prosecutor may hope, of course, that the jury will infer the stated conclusion from the evidence for the nonstated one. More often than not, however, missing the point occurs because of carelessness or because of the subtle unconscious prejudices of those involved in a particular argument.

Example: "The present method of evaluating public school teachers, which, at best, is an occasional perfunctory check by an administrator, is quite inadequate. If a teacher turns out to be a poor one, there is presently no effective way of getting rid of him or her. Therefore, teachers should be hired for a 'term of service,' after which they will reenter the job market, seeking jobs through the usual screening processes." There may be good reasons for hiring teachers for terms of service, but that conclusion does not follow from the evidence presented. A more relevant conclusion might be that some method of systematic evaluation should be found that would provide a defensible basis for discharging incompetent teachers.

Example: "Americans have a great heritage built on fine ideals. And we should all help to carry on this great heritage by passing it on to our children. That is why all Americans should regularly go to church on Sunday." In this argument, no evidence is given to show the connection between passing on our national heritage and going regularly to church. Such a connection could conceivably be established, but as we are provided with no evidence for it, the conclusion must be judged irrelevant.

Example: "The courts have been grossly unfair to newspaper reporters—forcing some of them to go to prison just because they wouldn't reveal the sources of their information. The reporters keep the public informed, and we all know that a well-informed public is necessary to bring about any semblance of justice. Besides, reporters keep public officials and others 'honest' by digging out the facts behind their claims, and exposing them when they don't tell the truth or when they engage in questionable practices." The weight of evidence in this argument supports the view that newspaper reporters perform a very useful and important service for their readers; it does not support the claim that the courts have been unfair to reporters. That particular conclusion misses the point of the evidence.

Attacking the Fallacy: An argument that misses the point can be very persuasive, for it sometimes gives good support for a particular thesis, although, unfortunately, it is not the one at issue. It might be well to point out what conclusion the evidence does support and to suggest that evidence for the *stated* conclusion is still needed if that conclusion is to be justified.

Because your opponent usually will not easily agree to the charge that his or her premises and conclusion are irrelevant to one another, it will probably be necessary to explain just how they are irrelevant. This will be especially true if the issue involved is one about which the speaker has strong feelings. Don't simply dismiss the conclusion! That will very likely only alienate your opponent. A better approach might be to offer your help in developing premises that are supportive of the conclusion. If the two of you together are unsuccessful, the questionableness of the conclusion should become clear.

Genetic Fallacy

Definition: This fallacy consists in evaluating a thing in terms of its earlier context and then carrying over that evaluation to the thing in the present.

The genetic fallacy occurs when one attempts to reduce the significance of an idea, person, practice, or institution merely to an account of its origin (genesis) or its earlier forms, thereby overlooking the development, regression, or difference to be found in it in the present situation. One who commits this fallacy typically transfers the positive or negative esteem that he or she has for the thing in its original context or earlier forms to the thing in its present form.

Example: "You're not going to wear a wedding ring, are you? Don't you know that the wedding ring originally symbolized the ankle chains worn by women to prevent them from running away from their husbands? I would not have thought you would be a party to such a sexist practice." There may be reasons why people may not wish to wear wedding rings, but it would be logically inappropriate for a couple to reject the notion of exchanging wedding rings on the sole grounds of its sexist origins.

Example: The genetic fallacy is sometimes committed by fundamentalist ministers and others who forbid certain practices on the basis of their supposed origins. For example, it is sometimes asserted that "a good Christian" should not dance, because dancing was originally used in pagan mystery cults as a way of worshipping pagan gods. Though there could be good reasons to argue against some forms of dance, the alleged genesis of the dance is not one of them.

Example: "I wouldn't vote for Jim Clinard for anything. You see, I grew up with him. We went to grade school together. He was just one big goof-off. You couldn't depend upon him for anything. I shudder to think of his being governor of any state in which I lived." The speaker here is assuming that Clinard is the same kind of person now that he was when he was in grade school. The speaker overlooks the possibility that Clinard may have matured or changed into quite a different person than he was then.

Attacking the Fallacy: Getting an arguer to disregard the origin or original context of an idea or thing is not easy. Strong emotional responses connected to those origins are particularly difficult to dismiss. Consider, for example, how difficult it might be to evaluate objectively the attractiveness of one of your spouse's suits or dresses that was selected by a former mate. Where a thing comes from does tend to have a rather potent effect upon the way we evaluate it. Nevertheless, it is methodologically important to try to dismiss such factors in our deliberations about their worth. When someone fails to dismiss such considerations, it would be appropriate to ask what there is about the thing *itself* that he or she finds either objectionable or worthwhile. If necessary, you might ask something like this: "Would your relationship to your mate be altered in any way if you discovered that your first date was not based on mutual attractiveness but was part of an elaborate practical joke?" It is my assumption that, though one might have very negative feelings toward such an unflattering beginning to the romance, he or she would regard the quality of its origin as irrelevant to the present quality of the relationship. Relationships, like ideas, people, and institutions, *change,* and former evaluations of them or their origins are not usually relevant considerations.

Assigning Irrelevant Functions or Goals

Definition: This fallacy consists in criticizing a policy or program because it does not or would not achieve certain goals that it was never designed to or expected to achieve.

Almost any program, policy, or piece of legislation has certain limited functions or goals that its designers quite readily recognize. Moreover, few programs, when implemented, are such that their most ideal consequences can be or are expected to be fulfilled. Therefore, when these ideal consequences are not fulfilled, it is not a sufficient justification for abandoning the program. This is especially true if the program has the effect of accomplishing some important goal or performing some important function that otherwise probably would not be brought about.

Example: The following is a summary of a typical conversation between many a college philosophy major and his or her critics:

Lynn: Do you really think that philosophy will ever solve all of our problems?
Owen: No, probably not.
Lynn: Then why are you wasting your time studying it?

What the critic fails to recognize is that no philosopher would ever claim that philosophy can solve all human problems. The philosopher simply claims that philosophical inquiry can be very effective in helping us to solve many of our problems. There would be no justification for abandoning it simply because it is not effective in helping us to solve all our problems.

Example: Many critics of gun-control legislation have argued that, because gun-control laws probably will not prevent criminals from using guns in the course of committing crimes, there is no good reason to pass such legislation. As far as the control of crimes is concerned, the proponents of gun-control legislation recognize that it can probably have only limited effect. Indeed, the serious criminal will probably not be much affected by the restricted sale and registration of guns, but the legislation could serve other very important functions, such as making guns less readily available as a means for settling domestic quarrels. Moreover, gun control might have the effect of reducing the number of accidental killings. Hence, in spite of its limitations, proponents think that there are still very good reasons for passing legislation that would control gun use.

Example: "Certainly you're not considering buying that gymsuit; it doesn't look the least bit becoming on you." Gymsuits are not designed primarily to look becoming; they serve other quite different functions—namely, to be comfortable, to allow relatively unrestricted physical activity, and to withstand extreme stress.

Attacking the Fallacy: One way of helping to prevent a fallacious response to your own proposal or program is to make every effort to specify its limited goals. It might even be helpful to remind your listener of your awareness of such limitations as often as possible. Such reminders would tend to disarm the critic who wished to make a program more vulnerable to attack by assigning it irrelevant functions. The critic may thereby be prevented from taking a "cheap shot" at the program. If the critic persists, make it clear that he or she is attacking a claim that no one is making or that a misrepresentation of the claim is being attacked.

Abusive *Ad Hominem*

Definition: This fallacy consists in attacking one's opponent in a personal and abusive way rather than responding to the claim or argument.

An *ad hominem* argument is an argument directed "toward the person," even though the character, behavior, or other personal characteristics of that person are, in most cases, irrelevant to the merits of his or her argument or claim. Even so, many people really do believe that they are making a forceful argument against their opponents' beliefs when they attack their opponents in personal ways. In one sense, of course, the abusive *ad hominem* argument is very forceful; it often has a persuasive effect in that it tends to discredit one's opponent or at least make him or her look ridiculous. If the opponent has some personal characteristic that is particularly distasteful to a listener, focusing attention upon it can be a very effective means of blunting the force of the argument. Even though the abusive claims about one's opponent may be true, those facts are irrelevant to the worth of his or her point of view, for even the most despicable of persons may be able to construct sound arguments.

Example:

Sara: Professor Elliott gave an excellent lecture last night on the creative process as it is related to sculpture. You should have been there!

Phillip: I have no interest in Professor Elliott's opinions. I'd be surprised if any piece of her sculpture has ever even "placed" in an art show. Have you ever seen any of her junk?

The fact that Professor Elliott may not be a particularly good sculptor is not significantly relevant to a judgment about her scholarly insights concerning the creative process.

Example: "No wonder you think promiscuity is all right. You know you've never had a really good relationship with a woman. So it's not strange that you'd resort to recreational sex." An opponent's judgment about the moral appropriateness of nonexclusive sexual relations should be evaluated apart from any consideration of his or her own particular sexual behavior or experience.

Example:

Cynthia: Professor Sanders says that cleaning up the environment should be our first priority if we are going to survive to the twenty-first century.

Denise: What does he know? He doesn't even keep his own *clothes* clean. He's been wearing the same filthy clothes for the last two weeks.

Denise is responding not to Professor Sanders' claim about the issue of making a clean environment a top priority, but to Professor Sanders' personal habits, which are not relevant to the merit of his claim, although Denise might like Cynthia to infer that they are. Even if there *were* an inconsistency between his behavior and his claim, that inconsistency would not be relevant to the evaluation of his claim.[1]

Attacking the Fallacy: Perhaps the best way to confront an abusive *ad hominem* argument is to concentrate on not becoming angered or at least on not expressing any anger. When we are abusively attacked, there is a great temptation to counterattack in the same abusive way. If we yield to that temptation, listeners will love it, but such a tactic will not help to advance the debate on the real issue. Indeed, it could slow it down considerably. In spite of the fact that we often feel helpless when abused or ridiculed, the most constructive thing to do is to point out to an opponent that he or she is being abusive and then politely ask for a response to the *argument*.

Circumstantial *Ad Hominem*

Definition: This fallacy consists in urging an opponent to accept a particular position by appealing to his or her special circumstances or self-interest.

This *ad hominem* argument is also directed "toward the person," but in this case the argument appeals to an opponent's personal or special circumstances as a means of persuasion. However, one's special circumstances rarely constitute a relevant, let alone a sufficient, reason for accepting or rejecting an assertion or an idea.

---

[1]For an expanded discussion of this issue, see the section on *tu quoque* argument, pp. 83–84.

Example: "I really don't see how you can favor no-fault automobile insurance. A large part of your law firm's business comes from cases involving auto accidents. In fact, I wouldn't be surprised if it weren't accident-related cases that are keeping us lawyers in business." One lawyer is here attempting to appeal to another on the basis of the other's self-interest. No consideration at all is given to the worth of the program of no-fault insurance itself.

Example: "Nancy, I would have thought that you would be actively supporting an affirmative action program here at the university. Because you're a woman, you of all people should see the merit of using every means available to hire more women to work in areas that have traditionally been dominated by men." The special circumstance that Nancy is a woman is not a relevant or sufficient reason for her to support such a program. Whatever her reason for not actively supporting affirmative action, being a woman is not a relevant consideration in the determination of her judgment.

Example: The following circumstantial *ad hominem* argument is used by one faculty member to gain another's vote in an important curriculum fight: "Don't you realize, Professor Morris, that if we drop the foreign language requirement, very few of our students will be likely to take a foreign language? And if your Latin courses can't pull enough students on their own, there's no way the college could justify keeping you on." The question of whether a foreign language should be required of all students should be determined on the basis of factors relevant to the requirement. The fact that it provides a job for Professor Morris should be irrelevant.

Attacking the Fallacy: It is ironic that some of the same people who present us with circumstantial *ad hominem* arguments based on self-interest think it unscrupulous when we accept or reject some other proposal on the basis of self-interest. It would seem, therefore, that people who use such appeals are probably aware, in their more reflective moments, that personal circumstances constitute no relevant reason for accepting or rejecting an idea. If someone confronts you with such an appeal, you might apply a kind of reversibility criterion by asking whether such considerations would still be relevant if they led you to an alternative or contrary point of view. If you wish to head the debate in a more positive direction, you might ask the user of the circumstantial *ad hominem* what he or she considers good reasons, apart from those related to personal circumstances, for supporting the position at issue.

Poisoning the Well

Definition: This fallacy consists in rejecting a claim defended by another because of that person's special circumstances or improper motives or because of a negative evaluation of that person.

This fallacy is called poisoning the well because its effect is to discredit the source of a particular argument or point of view in such a way that it precludes any consideration of the merit of that position. In other words, it "damns the source" in such a way that nothing that comes from that source will be or can be regarded as worthy of serious consideration. Even if a charge about someone's special circumstances or questionable motives were true in a particular case, that fact would not contribute to any disproof of the claim at issue. The truth of a claim or the worthiness of a course of action can in no way be inferred from the motives or personal circumstances of the defender of that claim.

A special case of poisoning the well is exhibited when one rejects an idea simply because of one's negative evaluation of the person presenting it. To avoid committing this fallacy, it is necessary to separate a strong dislike of a person from appreciation of his or her comments or ideas.

Example: "You're not a woman, so anything you might say about abortion is of no significance." The special circumstance of not being a woman should not preclude a male from presenting a position on the question of abortion that is worthy of serious consideration.

Example: Several years ago, at a public symposium on alienation held at Emory & Henry College, Howard Fuller, a black militant, refused to listen to the integrationist-oriented remarks of well-known philosopher Sidney Hook. Fuller said: "You're not a black man, so anything you have to say on the subject of black alienation is of no interest to me. You just can't know what you're talking about." Professor Hook's well had been effectively poisoned. Anything that he had to say was regarded as tainted in Fuller's mind, and after Fuller's attack, anything that Hook had to say was regarded as tainted in the thinking of many members of the symposium audience.

Example: In reference to the Woodward-Bernstein Watergate reports in the *Washington Post,* it was said at the time: "The so-called evidence against President Nixon shouldn't be taken too seriously, because it was obviously put together by reporters out to make a name for themselves." No doubt any reporter would like to make a name, but that motivation does not necessarily taint the evidence he or she might discover in support of a particular claim.

Attacking the Fallacy: It is sometimes quite difficult to attack the poisoning the well fallacy, especially if it is *your* well that has been poisoned, because even your attack upon such reasoning supposedly comes from a contaminated source. In the abortion example above, as long as you are a male, any response on your part may be regarded with suspicion. Perhaps the most constructive thing to do in such cases would be to confront the issue directly: "Okay, you've poisoned my well, so that anything I say is suspect. That is a very effective device, and there's not a whole lot that I can do about it. But I do not intend to be silenced so easily. One reason you might want to silence me is that you think that what I say might seriously damage your position. I think I *do* have something significant to say, and I'd be interested in your response to it." It is possible, of course, that such a forceful response will not be necessary, for you may find some way of convincing your opponent that there can be no real debate if there is only one speaker.

Tu Quoque Argument

Definition: This fallacy consists in responding to an attack on one's ideas or actions by accusing one's critic or others of thinking or acting in a similar way or a way that is equally hard to defend.

If there is one fallacy that, in ordinary experience, does not strike most of us as fallacious, it is this one. Most all children feel entirely justified in antisocial behavior if they can respond to the scolding parent: "But he (or she) did it first." Moreover, most adults tend to feel absolved of any guilt for their behavior if they can say to a critic: "You do the same thing!" The very name of the fallacy, *tu quoque*, translates as "You [do it] too." Even though most of us would agree that "two wrongs don't make a right," when our own behavior is questioned, it almost always seems to make us feel better if we can point out that our critic, or some other person, acts in a similar way. But there is no logical way that another's fault can absolve our own guilt for the same fault, nor does the behavior of another person or group constitute any logical justification for us to behave in a similar manner. Not all users of the *tu quoque* argument, however, are trying to absolve their guilt; some use it as a diversionary tactic to draw attention away from their own questionable behavior.

A common experience is the desire to point out the inconsistencies between what a critic says and what he or she does; in other words, we commonly expect a person to "practice what he or she preaches." However, the inconsistency between what we say and what we do is in no way relevant to the merits of our criticism of another person. If we apply certain principles, rules, or criteria to the judgments or actions of another person while failing or refusing to apply them to ourselves or to a situation that especially interests us, we may be legitimately accused of "special pleading"—that is, making a special case of ourselves—or even of hypocrisy; but any negative judgment against us would probably be a moral one rather than a logical one.

Example:

Father: Owen, I really don't think that you should be drinking. Alcohol tends to dull your senses, reduces your physical control, and may even become psychologically addicting.
Son: That's not a very convincing argument, Dad, when you're standing there with that martini in your hand.

Although it might be tempting for Owen to point out to his father the apparent inconsistency between what he is saying and what he is doing, the proper action is to respond to the merit of his argument. In this case, Owen could attack with relevant evidence the claim about the effects of alcohol consumption, or he could accept the claim, if it were supported by the evidence, and perhaps adjust his behavior accordingly.

Example:

Thurman: At your age, you really shouldn't work so hard, Roy. You're going to completely exhaust yourself and end up in the hospital.
Roy: You work just as hard as I do, Thurman, and you are not one bit younger than I am.

Roy has not really responded to Thurman's claim that, if he continues to work at the same level, he might develop some serious physical problems. Instead, he has used the *tu quoque* argument as a means of drawing attention away from himself.

Example: Suppose that the golf pro tells you in your first golf lesson that the first and most important thing to do in learning to become an effective golfer is "to keep your head down and your eye on the ball." It would be fallacious to conclude that you are not being given sound advice, simply because the golf pro doesn't always keep her head down when she plays tournament golf.

Attacking the Fallacy: Perhaps the best way of preparing yourself for confronting the *tu quoque* argument is to resist the strong temptation to commit it yourself. Even if an arguer defends a particular principle in arguing against your position and then denies that principle in an argument supporting his or her own position, you could not legitimately accuse that person of committing a fallacy. An evaluation of any particular argument should be confined to that argument alone.

If an inconsistency between what you yourself say and do is discovered, do not be intimidated or silenced by such a charge. Simply admit the truth of the charge and go on with your argument, insisting that your verbal opponent evaluate *its* merits. Moreover, if your opponent points out an inconsistency between what you claim in one argument and what you claim in another, you will no doubt wish to resolve the problem as quickly and as carefully as possible, so that he or she will not be distracted from evaluating the merits of whichever argument is at hand.

When charged with *tu quoque* reasoning, the arguer will probably acknowledge its faulty character. Not many people would defend, in principle, the view that "two wrongs make a right" or that improper behavior by one person justifies similar behavior by another. However, because *tu quoque* reasoning is usually more emotional than logical, it is not usually fully recognized until it is brought to one's attention.

Exercises

A. Identify the type of fallacy of irrelevance in each of the following:

1. **A:** I've gone off my diet. It just isn't working.
   B: But I thought it was working real well. Haven't you already lost about twenty pounds?

A: Sure, I've lost weight, but my social life hasn't improved one bit!

2. I don't see any reason why we should hire a person with a Ph.D. to fill this position in our department. Many people *without* Ph.D.s are much better teachers than people *with* Ph.D.s. Getting a Ph.D. doesn't make one a better teacher.

3. I really can't take your arguments very seriously, son. A 16-year-old just hasn't lived long enough to know what life is all about.

4. I just don't understand why you are opposing federal aid to parochial schools. Both of us are Catholics who are committed to the parochial school concept, and you know our schools are badly in need of financial resources. If this bill for financial assistance to parochial schools doesn't pass the Congress, it will probably mean that many of our schools will have to close their doors.

5. A: The most practical reason for not smoking marijuana is simply that it's illegal.

B: Don't talk to me about obeying the law! You rarely drive within the legal speed limit, and most of the time you have more than the legal limit of alcohol in your system.

6. Don't tell me how to raise my children! I don't care how much you've studied child psychology; if you don't have any children of your own, you can't possibly understand kids.

7. Professor A: I think that the practice of giving special academic awards and honors to students on so-called honors day does nothing but build a recipient's ego. It doesn't help him or her to do any better academically. It serves *no* positive function, as far as I can see.

Professor B: Well, I notice you didn't turn down your Phi Beta Kappa award at college. You've got your certificate there on the wall behind you, just as big as life. You even framed it in black to make it stand out.

8. Grades don't really give us much information about a student. If a prospective employer or graduate school were to find from a transcript that a student got a B− in a particular course, very little could be inferred about the particular character or quality of his or her work in that course. Hence I think that we ought to go to a simple Pass-Fail system.

9. Candidate Phillips: My political opponent, Representative Abbott, is not telling the truth when he says that he has never missed a single roll-call vote in the House of Representatives during his long tenure. According to the *Congressional Record*, Mr. Abbott missed 23 percent of the roll-call votes during his first term.

Representative Abbott: Ms. Phillips, is the *Congressional Record* the only piece of reading material that they would allow you to read at the mental hospital in which you were a patient during my first term?

10. No, I do not intend to support Senator Kennedy's health-care bill. I've never had any use for the Kennedys, so I do not intend to lend my support to a Kennedy cause.

B. From among all the fallacies studied to this point, choose the fallacy that most closely resembles the problem exhibited in each of the following:

11. A: Just stop yelling at me! The only way that we're ever going to solve any problem is to sit down and talk calmly about it. Screaming at me will not help in any way!
B: Well, you don't yell! You just cry all the time! Do you think that's any better?

12. Are you now or have you ever been a member of the Communist Party?

13. I know that the sign says that the safe speed for these curves is 25 miles per hour, but if 25 miles per hour is safe, then 30 miles an hour shouldn't give me any problem. After all, there's not a whole lot of difference between 25 and 30 miles per hour.

14. The recently instituted "no-knock" policy of metropolitan police departments should be abandoned, because it has not at all reduced the number of crimes committed in our major cities.

15. Radio preacher: "We must judge this issue by what the Bible *says*, not by what we think it says or by what some scholar or theologian thinks it says."

16. King James I of England argued against republicanism in the following way: "If you cut off the head of a body, the other organs cannot function, and the body dies. Similarly, if you cut off the head of the state (the King), the state may flop around for a while, but it will eventually die."

17. About the same time that I began drinking heavily, my grades began to go down. I guess that heavy drinking and good grades just don't mix.

18. No, I don't want my boys to join the Boy Scouts. Did you know that the Boy Scouts were organized as a paramilitary organization? They even trained the young boys in accordance with a military scouting manual. The "scouts" in "Boy Scouts" literally refers to *military* scouts. None of my children is going to join such an organization with my blessing.

19. Presidential candidate in a television interview: "We're going to win this election. We've got the spirit, the determination, and the confidence—and most important of all, we believe in ourselves."

20. If Buchanan is elected to the county board, you can count on him to keep down the tax rate on property. His opponent, Mr. Groseclose, wants to increase substantially the number of county services, and that's going to take a lot more money. With as much property as *you* have, there should be no question about whom you should vote for.

VII
Irrelevant Appeals

The fallacies discussed in this chapter make specific appeals to factors that are irrelevant in sound reasoning. One particular classification of these irrelevant appeals involves an appeal to human emotions. In such cases emotions are used as a substitute for evidence, to attract attention away from weak evidence, and to play upon the particular feelings of the people to whom an argument is addressed. A second type of irrelevant appeal involves a misuse of appeal to authority. Such appeals use irrelevant or at least highly questionable "authorities" in support of their claims.

Appeal to Pity

Definition: This fallacy consists in attempting to persuade others of one's point of view by appealing to their sympathy instead of presenting evidence.

The prospect that someone may be disappointed or suffer some kind of mental anguish by your failure to give a desired response to a claim or proposal is usually an irrelevant consideration in the determination of the merit of the claim or proposal. One who appeals to pity is actually attempting to get you to "give in" to or accept the claim at issue rather than to persuade you that the claim is true or has merit; that is, he or she is exploiting your emotional sensitivities rather than presenting you with convincing evidence.

Of course, there may be some situations where the potential hurt to others is a relevant consideration in adopting or rejecting a proposal. In such cases, however, it should be made clear just why it is relevant. If it cannot be shown to be importantly relevant, it should play no significant role in the acceptance or rejection of an idea.

In the context of moral reasoning, in which there is a normative premise employed, it is quite possible that an appeal to pity would not be fallacious. Indeed, it could be used very effectively as a device to draw attention to a moral principle used in the argument.[1] However, in a context in which no such moral premise is used, an appeal that exploits one's vague feelings of generosity or concern for others while neglecting (or at least obscuring) a more relevant principle or issue at stake is probably fallacious.

A number of critics have suggested that, if there is a fallacy of appeal to pity, it involves coming to some *belief* on the basis of pity rather than on the basis of evidence. They doubt whether the appeal to pity is fallacious when it involves a decision about a course of action, because, as they say, such decisions often involve "moral considerations." I contend, however, that very few people ever come to *believe* something to be *true* simply on the basis of pity. The typical case in which the fallacious appeal to pity is used is in persuading persons toward a particular course of action—without explicit or even implicit reference to a defensible moral principle.

Example: "Larry, I really think that you ought to take Nikki to the May dance next Friday. She hasn't had a date all year. In fact, she has never been invited to go to any dance. Have you ever thought what it might be like to sit alone in your room every time there is a campus dance, while all your friends are doing what you'd like to be doing?" Larry may truly feel sorry for Nikki. As he imagines what it might be like for Nikki or someone like her, he might even wish that she could be relieved of such hurt. However, such feelings should not be given weighty consideration in his response to the suggestion that he invite Nikki to the dance. A nonfallacious argument for inviting Nikki should provide evidence that spending the evening with Nikki would be a pleasant or enjoyable experience. If he took Nikki because he felt sorry for her, he would be doing it for the wrong reasons.

Example: The sympathies that may be aroused by the fact that someone has a physical handicap should not play a primary role in a decision to hire that person. Even though your sympathies may be further aroused by the fact that he or she has had great difficulty getting a job, partly because of the handicap, that too does not constitute a good reason for hiring. The most relevant consideration in hiring someone usually has to do with which person is best qualified for the job or will most likely do the best job in the position.

Example: If you owned an apartment house and one of your older tenants were three months behind in rent payments, you might indeed be emotionally upset by the task of asking her to move out. If the tenant argued she had no place to go, had no relatives, and had no money, that plea would probably arouse some pity in any decent human being; but it should not constitute a significant factor in the

[1]You should not assume, of course, that your own moral principles are shared by one to whom you address your argument. Even in cases where such principles may be shared, they may not be relevant to the substance of the issue at stake.

decision to evict or not to evict the tenant. The primary purpose for owning an apartment house is usually earning some profit on an investment. A nonpaying tenant violates that primary function.

Attacking the Fallacy: If you allow yourself to be overcome by the force of an emotional appeal, it is important to remember that you are no less guilty of fallacious reasoning than the one who formulates the appeal. You have allowed the description or projection of a pitiable situation to count as evidence, even though, in most cases, it does not constitute any evidence at all. However, in order to avoid appearing to be an insensitive brute, it might be well to acknowledge your aroused feelings openly, yet to state specifically that you are not going to allow them to interfere with the process of coming to a defensible judgment. You might also point out that to respond positively to a proposal primarily because of those feelings would be to respond, in most cases, for the wrong reasons. Then ask the arguer if there are any other reasons why the proposal merits your acceptance.

Appeal to the Gallery

Definition: This fallacy consists in attempting to persuade others of one's point of view by appealing to their strong emotions or to popular sentiments instead of presenting evidence for one's view.

The "gallery" to which an appeal is made refers to the undiscriminating public, which is often easily swayed through a manipulation of their strong feelings. Another name for this fallacy might be appeal to strong or popular sentiments or appeal to the crowd. Some of the strong emotions to which appeals are often made are fear, ethnic and social superiority, greed, and shame. Positive sentiments that are often exploited are familial concerns, patriotism, national security, group loyalty, and military superiority. Popular feelings against such groups as labor unions, certain religious or political associations, homosexuals, or even radical college students have also been manipulated as a means of persuasion. The arguer's choice of which sentiment to exploit is, of course, determined by the constituency of the gallery.

There are several distinctive types of appeal to the gallery that deserve special attention. One very effective way of persuading others is to flatter them in some manner. For example, you have probably heard a speaker say something like this: "Because you are a mature audience of highly educated professionals, I'm sure that you can see clearly the merit of my proposal." Excessive praise, of course, is not fallacious by itself. It only becomes fallacious if it is used as a substitute for evidence. A second distinctive type of appeal to the gallery is the appeal to shame. It seeks to elicit a feeling of guilt from a person or group for holding an unpopular opinion or for acting in a particular way, without demonstrating why guilt would be warranted. A third type of gallery appeal involves the manipulation of negative feelings, by pointing out that the opposing view is held by people or groups with negative prestige. This appeal encourages one to accept the arguer's position in order to avoid any guilt by association with those held in negative esteem. A fourth type of this appeal involves group loyalty. It attempts to persuade a person to accept a position because of his or her identification with a particular social group that accepts the point of view in question. Such loyalty, however, is a questionable consideration in determining the truth of a claim or in choosing a course of action.

Example: The fact that the platform of the Republican Party supports an antiabortion amendment to the U.S. Constitution does not constitute a good reason for Senator Davis, a six-term Republican Senator, to support that amendment. Loyalty to one's political affiliates should not play any significant role in the formulation of one's position on such an issue. Hence, an appeal based upon that consideration would probably be an irrelevant one. A proper appeal would focus on possible reasons such an amendment might be needed.

Example: Representative Fisher was clearly appealing to the gallery in this floor speech in the House: "We should definitely discontinue our wheat sales to the Russian 'commies.' If we sell our wheat to them, we'll be helping to prop up a communist dictatorship and deliberately aiding our worst enemy. We cannot gain, we can only lose; for we would be encouraging the growth of a society opposed in every way to our own and thereby increasing the threat to our own security." Representative Fisher's appeal to anticommunist sentiment is irrelevant to the substantive issue involved. A sounder argument would have included evidence that the wheat sales would work an economic hardship upon ordinary American citizens, unfavorably affect the U.S. import-export balance, or have an unhealthy effect upon the national economy.

Example: Notice how Professor Smith attempts to manipulate the negative feelings of Professor Jackson in the following exchange:

Professor Smith: You are going to vote with *us* on this issue at next week's faculty meeting, aren't you?
Professor Jackson: No, I really don't think it is a very good idea.
Professor Smith: Really? Well, neither does Professor Hart or Professor Carter. They're voting against us too.

If Professors Hart and Carter are people with whom Professor Jackson has always disagreed or predictably opposes, it is possible that he might be tempted to alter his opinion. At least that is what Professor Smith hopes will happen. However, as no relevant evidence was presented for Professor Jackson's consideration, there is no relevant reason for him to move over to Professor Smith's position.

Attacking the Fallacy: Appeals to the gallery are most effective when they are directed toward the uniformed or the uncritical, but even some of the most reflective people can be influenced by appeals to their own subtle prejudices, loyalties, and lifestyles. Even though you might candidly admit to some of these irrational or indefensible preferences, you should make every effort not to allow them to intrude upon the process of making a careful judgment about an issue.

Not only should you take care not to allow yourself to be moved by appeals based on strong sentiments, you should also not allow speakers who appeal to the gallery to think that they have offered any relevant reason in support of a claim. There are several ways in which this might be done. First, you could simply inform your opponent that you are unable to properly evaluate or respond to the claim unless more *relevant* evidence is offered in support of it. Second, if your own sentiments correspond with those expressed by your opponent, you might freely admit that fact. Such an admission would probably have a somewhat disarming effect upon the arguer. But you should hasten to inform him or her that you do not intend to allow your feelings to obstruct your careful scrutiny of the issue. In other words, you should make it clear that you have *not* been convinced and are still waiting to be convinced on the basis of relevant evidence. Third, you could use an example or two to give an additional thrust to your attack. You might point out that even though one's loyalties may be with the home football team, those feelings should not prevent one from recognizing the superior abilities of the rival team. Likewise, one's extremely negative feelings toward Russian spies should not play an important role in evaluating the wisdom or propriety of the Soviet Union's maintaining an effective espionage system in behalf of its national security and other vital interests, especially in view of the elaborate espionage system maintained by the United States in behalf of its national security and other vital interests.

Appeal to Force or Threat

Definition: This fallacy consists in attempting to persuade others of one's point of view by threatening them with some undesirable state of affairs instead of presenting evidence for one's view.

Unfortunately, such intimidation can often gain acceptance of a conclusion in the absence of a convincing argument. There is nothing wrong, of course, with pointing out the consequences of a particular course of action. In fact, if certain consequences are a natural outcome of an action, calling attention to them might be very much appreciated. In some such cases, being aware of the consequences of an action might even cause one to alter one's course. However, if an arguer tries to force another to accept the truth of a claim or the rightness of an action by threatening some undesirable action, then the arguer is guilty of using an irrelevant appeal.

One particular form of this fallacy is often referred to as *authoritarianism*. Authoritarianism consists in appealing to someone as an authority not because of that person's skill, knowledge, or expertise in a field but because of his or her power or influence over the one to whom the argument is directed. In such a case, a demand for blind submission to that authority takes the place of relevant evidence or good reasons.

Example: "Sure, you can unionize the shop, but I won't be responsible if you are permanently unemployed afterward." The employer here is not so subtly threatening employees. The course of action that he or she wants them to accept is not unionizing the shop. However, the appropriateness of not unionizing is not defended with good reasons; the employer has used instead a method designed to intimidate the employees into submission.

Example: The following exchange illustrates a familiar example of authoritarian thinking:

> **Sean:** Dad, why do I have to go to church every Sunday?
> **Father:** Because I'm your father, and I say so, that's why.

Sean is asking what good reasons there are for attending church, but his father responds by demanding blind obedience to his will. The father, in this case, is appealing to his power over the boy to force his compliance. His alleged argument is fallacious, for it offers no relevant reasons for attending church.

Example: One of the most effective appeals of many religious fundamentalists in reaching possible converts is the threat of eternal damnation. "Burning in hell" is not a relevant reason for accepting the truth or the rightness of the Christian faith. It may be that many people do accept it as true because of their fears, but the prospect of dire personal consequences following upon the rejection of a particular religious perspective is not relevant to its truth.

Attacking the Fallacy: It is sometimes difficult to withstand the pressure of a threat, particularly when it comes, as it usually does, from someone with the power to place you in a very undesirable situation. Indeed, your ability or inclination to reject such irrelevant appeals may depend upon your own sense of personal, economic, and professional security. Nevertheless, I suggest that one who is guilty of appealing to force or threat should at the least be exposed. One way of doing this might be to say to such a person: "I know what you're going to do to me if I don't accept your position, but are there any good reasons for believing it to be *true* or *right*?"

Appeal to Tradition

Definition: This fallacy consists in attempting to persuade others of one's point of view by appealing to their feelings of reverence or respect for some tradition that supports that view rather than presenting appropriate evidence.

Emotional attachments to the past are common and pleasant experiences for almost all of us. The comfortable feeling that we have with a particular traditional way of acting or thinking may be one reason we revere it, but it is not a reason for regarding it as true or as the best way of doing things. Indeed, the English philosopher John Stuart Mill claimed that "the despotism of custom is everywhere the standing hindrance to human advancement." A comfortable feeling is not a suitable substitute for evidence or good reasons. Moreover, even though most traditions might originally have had good reasons behind them, those reasons may no longer be relevant.

Example: "Nancy, if you keep your maiden name after you marry, you'll run into all kinds of problems. People will think you're making a big fuss over nothing. Besides, a woman who loves her husband has always been proud to be called by his name. In our culture, taking a husband's last name is what makes a woman really feel married." In this argument, no good reason other than tradition is given for a woman to adopt her husband's last name. There may be some very good reasons to continue that practice rather than for each partner to maintain his or her own name, yet the arguer makes no use of them. The only alleged evidence is irrelevant to the issue at stake.

Example: "But, John, our family has always been Southern Baptist. Your grandfather was a Southern Baptist minister, and you have two uncles who are Southern Baptist ministers. Your mother's family has also always been Southern Baptist. I just don't understand how you could even *think* of joining the Methodist Church." John's father has pointed out several facts to John in order to impress upon him the family tradition. However, no ecclesiastical or theological considerations are given any attention at all—only feelings of reverence for a family tradition.

Example: "When I was in public school we had prayer every day at the beginning of the school session. It was a very meaningful thing for me. I just don't see why my children can't have the same kind of experience." No counterargument is offered here to the Supreme Court position that required prayer in public schools constitutes an "establishment of religion"; the only appeal is to the comfortableness of a tradition.

Attacking the Fallacy: Assure your verbal opponent that there is nothing intrinsically wrong with doing things in a traditional way. In fact, you might even admit that you too often feel more comfortable with traditional ways of doing things. However, you should also point out that when there are good reasons for changing a way of acting or thinking or for not continuing a particular practice, then reverence for the past is an irrelevant consideration in the process of determining the future.

Irrelevant or Questionable Authority

Definition: This fallacy consists in attempting to support a claim by quoting the judgment of one who is not an authority in the field, the judgment of an unidentified authority, or the judgment of an authority who is likely to be significantly biased in some way.

An authority in a given field has been described as one who is in a position to have access to the facts he or she claims to know, is qualified by training or ability to draw appropriate inferences from those facts, and is free from any relevant prejudices or involvements that would prevent him or her from formulating sound judgments or communicating them truthfully and completely.[2] It is almost always appropriate to appeal to the judgment of such an authority as a means of supporting some claim when the authority's judgment is indeed based upon the facts and the facts are *adequate* to justify the judgment. It is only when the "authority" on whose judgment the argument rests fails to meet the stated criteria that the argument should be regarded as fallacious.

The fallacious appeal to authority occurs most frequently in the form of a transfer of an authority's competence from one field to another. An entertainer or athlete, for example, is appealed to as an authority on automobile mufflers or panty-hose; a nuclear scientist is called upon to support some religious claim; or a statesman is treated as an expert on marriage and the family. Indeed, the judgment of a famous and highly respected person is likely to be indiscriminately invoked on *any* subject. How often, for example, are the judgments of Socrates, Jesus, or Abraham Lincoln seriously questioned, regardless of what the subject matter happens to be?

An unidentified authority is questionable because there is no way for the listener to determine whether the unnamed authority is in fact a qualified one. Another type of improper authority is a biased one. Some people may be qualified in a particular field by training, ability, and position, yet they are so vitally affected by or "interested" in an arguer's conclusion that there would be good reason to treat their testimony with suspicion.

Example: "It's not true that the government is innocent of any wrongdoing with regard to pollution. I read the other day that the government itself is responsible for over 50 percent of the country's water pollution." Though it may be true that the U.S. Government is in some sense responsible for 50 percent of our water pollution, there is no reason to believe such a claim because the source of the claim is as yet unidentified. It should be clear that it is not the speaker's honesty that is being questioned, although his or her memory could possibly be faulty. The appeal is fallacious because the listener is not in a position to evaluate the qualifications of the source.

Example: "Senator, if you think that the F.B.I. has been engaging in unauthorized or illegal activities, why don't we get the Director and his staff over here at this hearing and get to the bottom of this thing? Who is in a better position to testify about F.B.I. operations than the Director and his division heads?" The appeal to authority here would be a most proper one in most inquiries concerning F.B.I. operations; yet such testimony might be questionable if the inquiry were intended to evaluate claims of wrongdoing within the Bureau that could in some way involve the Director himself.

Example: "I don't see how we can chance cutting the defense budget one penny more. According to Reverend Samples, our minister, all the signs on the

[2]Monroe Beardsley, *Thinking Straight,* 3rd ed. (Englewood Cliffs, N.J.: Prentice-Hall, 1966, p. 215.

international military and political scene point to an all-out military confrontation with Russia in the very near future." It is not likely that Reverend Samples is in a position to obtain the facts that he claims to know, and it is even less likely that he has the training and ability to draw any sound inference from those facts.

Attacking the Fallacy: If an argument invokes an unidentified authority, a first step in attacking it may be to ask for the authority to be identified. If the arguer is able to do this, then you are in a position to evaluate that authority by the standard criteria. In determining whether an authority is biased, you must be careful not to disqualify a source too quickly by claiming that he or she is prejudiced, for in doing so, you may be committing a fallacy yourself—that of poisoning the well.[3] It is not difficult to find or fabricate some reason why the judgment of almost *any* authority might be biased, but such a charge should be registered against an authority who is otherwise qualified only when the bias is quite clear and might significantly impede the discovery of the truth. In other words, an argument is fallacious by virtue of being based on a biased authority only when very unusual circumstances of prejudice prevail.

Most important of all, do not be intimidated when great names and respected professions are used in support of various claims. William Shakespeare, Mark Twain, Abraham Lincoln, Will Rogers, Dwight Eisenhower, Carl Sandburg, and many other "famous" people were experts, if at all, in very limited ranges of subject matter.

Appeal to Public Opinion

Definition: This fallacy consists in urging the acceptance of a position simply on the ground that most or at least great numbers of people accept it.

Two other names sometimes given to this fallacy are bandwagon fallacy and *consensus gentium*. The bandwagon notion suggests that an idea or action must be true or good because "everyone" is accepting it or jumping on it as they would on a bandwagon. *Consensus gentium* is literally translated "consent of the people." If a claim or idea is accepted by a majority, we are often led to believe that it is true or worthy. However, the truth or merit of an idea is in no way dependent upon the number of people who support it. Nevertheless, we commonly infer that a film is a good one if there are long lines of people waiting to see it, or we infer that a restaurant serves good food if there are a great number of cars outside it. Remember, however, that crowds are not usually noted for sound judgments and that other factors could account for the long lines and the large number of cars.

Example: "I'm going to buy a copy of Gore Vidal's new book. It must be a good one; it's been at the top of the best-seller lists for ten weeks." Literary merit is not the only factor that could account for a book's being on the best-seller lists. Other factors might account for it quite easily. For example, the book might have been a Book-of-the-Month Club selection, or perhaps the publisher has a contract

[3]See pp. 81–83.

with a very effective public-relations firm. The book might be a piece of literary trash that nevertheless appeals to the nation's large number of unsophisticated readers. The point is that nothing about the book's quality can be inferred from the fact that large numbers of people buy or even read it.

Example: "Marijuana can't be all wrong; according to a recent Gallup survey published in yesterday's *Wall Street Journal,* more than 70 percent of all college students smoke it more or less regularly." The merits of smoking marijuana cannot be ascertained by taking a poll. Polls may indicate what people are thinking, doing, or anticipating doing, but very little regarding the truth or merit of an idea, claim, or action can be inferred from such surveys.

Example: "Former President Gerald Ford claimed that there was no agreement or understanding, prior to Nixon's resignation, with regard to a possible pardon for any crimes Mr. Nixon might have committed while he was in office. But very few people really believe that!" The truth about whether there was a prior agreement between Mr. Ford and Mr. Nixon is not a matter to be decided by a majority vote of the people. What the people *think* is the truth is irrelevant to what *is* actually the case.

Attacking the Fallacy: Because your verbal opponent regards public opinion as representing truth, ask if he or she would regard a "true" claim as false if public opinion were to shift to the other side. Although it is unlikely that anyone would consciously respond positively to such a question, you should be prepared to point out that such thinking could lead to the absurd conclusion that a claim is both true *and* false, depending upon when the people are surveyed; and that such thinking surely must be faulty in some way.

Exercises

A. Identify the type of irrelevant appeal in each of the following:

1. Ed, I just can't vote for him, even though I agree with what you say about the two candidates. It's just that we have always been Democrats. My father would turn over in his grave if I voted for a Republican.

2. Real estate broker: "You mean that after we flew you down here to Florida at no cost to you, put you up in a Miami Beach hotel for three days with all meals provided, took you on a Caribbean fishing trip, and took you to Disney World, you're not going to buy even *one* of our small lots?"

3. I really don't think that you should buy a Vega. Someone told me that Vegas have a very bad repair record.

4. Are you sure you want to openly oppose this new curricular proposal? You know that both the President and the Dean are pushing it pretty hard—and you don't have tenure yet!

5. If you don't marry me, our poor child will go through life without ever knowing who his father was or without having a normal family life. A boy needs a father, John! Please don't deprive him of that.

6. Incest *must* be wrong, because virtually every society, both past and present, has forbidden it in one form or another.

7. College senior to major professor: "I know that I haven't done very good work in your courses, but if you don't write me a good recommendation, there is no way that I can get into graduate school. Professor Letson, graduate school means a lot to me. I know that if I get into graduate school I'll do good work, and you won't be sorry that you helped me when I really needed it."

8. I do hope that you will make a sizable pledge to the United Charities Fund this year, Bill. You were the only member of the managerial staff that pledged less than $100 last year.

9. Professor to student: "I really think that you ought to take my course in aesthetics, Nancy. In fact, if you don't take it, I think that I would have very serious reservations about writing you a strong recommendation for graduate school in philosophy."

10. David, you can't be serious about going to Annapolis! Our family has *always* been army—your brother, your father, your uncles, and even your grandfather—all of them, as you well know, went to West Point.

B. From among all the fallacies studied to this point, choose the fallacy that most closely resembles the problem exhibited in each of the following·

11. A: Who is that fellow over there at the corner table?
  B: I think he's that Russian historian who is teaching here at the university this term.

12. But, officer, you shouldn't give me a parking ticket for parking here! People park here all the time and never get tickets. I myself have been parking here for several months and never once received a ticket. No one pays any attention to the "No Parking" sign in this alley.

13. A: I say that "once saved, always saved." A person who is once saved or redeemed cannot fall from grace, that is, fall away from the faith. I suppose that's why we Baptists differ from you Methodists.
  B: But *I* know some people who now have nothing to do with the church, speak ill of it, and hardly lead lives that would be considered saved or Christian, yet they *did* have experiences of salvation when they were in their early teens. Are you saying they have not fallen away from the faith?
  A: Well, if those people act as you say they do, they must not have been really saved in the first place.

14. The voters of Massachusetts overwhelmingly defeated a proposed gun-control law in the state, which proves that gun control is really a rotten idea.

15. My husband is being cared for in one of the best hospitals in the country. They use all the latest techniques there.

16. I really don't expect Major Brank to do a very effective job on this project. The army is notoriously inefficient.

17. Jimmy Carter was elected President in 1976 because Senator Mondale was his running mate. Mondale made the difference between winning and losing the election.

18. Parishioner to priest: "You've never been married, so why should I listen to your advice concerning my marital problems? How could you possibly know what you're talking about?"

19. Legal measures that would put some controls on corporate monopolies are clearly in the public interest, because the good of the community would be decidedly improved if we could find some legal way of preventing the total control of the production and distribution of a particular service or product by a single corporation.

20. This country is like a machine. No matter who operates it, it will behave in essentially the same way. So it really doesn't make any difference who is elected President.

VIII
Fallacies of Diversion

The fallacies discussed in this chapter do not necessarily involve faulty inference. They are primarily ways of maneuvering to a more advantageous or less embarrassing position by directing attention away from the actual point at issue in an argument. Although there are a great many different tactics of diversion used in argumentation, I have attempted to group them broadly into four types of action that can be taken against an argument: distorting it, attacking only its weaker supports or one of its minor points, drawing attention away from it to a side issue, or ridiculing it.

Distortion

Definition: This fallacy consists in stating an opponent's point of view or argument in a distorted form, usually for the purpose of making it easier to attack.

There are several different ways in which one may distort an opponent's argument or point of view. First, one may extend it beyond its original bounds by drawing inferences from it that are clearly unwarranted or unintended. Second, one may deliberately misrepresent the argument or state it in a perverted form by utilizing only a part of it, by paraphrasing it in carefully chosen words, or by subtly including one's own evaluation or commentary in it. Third, one may oversimplify. An opponent's complex argument can be made to look absurd when it is stated in a simplified form that leaves out important qualifications or subtle distinctions.

Example: Misrepresentation or deliberate distortion is a clever and typical technique of politicians. If a candidate for national office argues for a decrease in the national defense budget by suggesting that billions can be saved by cutting out much waste and mismanagement, his political opponent might respond: "My opponent wants to weaken our defense posture around the world by cutting our defense spending. A cut could only mean reduction of our forces in strategic defense positions in Europe and Asia. *I* say that America cannot become a second-rate military power and still keep her commitments abroad." This example shows not only how a position may be misrepresented but also how it may be distorted by unwarranted inferences. Cutting out waste in defense spending does not necessarily entail reductions of armed forces in Europe and Asia nor America's becoming a second-rate military power.

Example: A very clear case of distorting by drawing unwarranted inferences is seen in this short exchange between a proponent and an opponent of a plan to construct a nuclear power plant nearby.

> **Proponent:** Unless we construct a nuclear power plant in this area within the next ten years, we will not be able to meet the significantly growing demand for power.
>
> **Opponent:** What you're saying is that you couldn't care less what happens to the wildlife and plant life or even the human lives that might be harmed by the presence of nuclear radiation in this area.

The opponent has drawn an inference from the proponent's argument that is clearly unwarranted. In no way could one conclude from that argument that the proponent was unconcerned about the possible environmental dangers of erecting a nuclear power plant in a particular area. Indeed, it is possible that every precaution had been taken to insure that no such harm to living things would occur.

Example:

> **Debra:** In summary, let me say that, after doing careful and serious reflection on this matter, I must conclude that there is no logical, moral, or legal justification for discriminating against a person on the basis of sex. Therefore, I am wholeheartedly supporting the Equal Rights Amendment to the U.S. Constitution.
>
> **Joe:** Look, if you want men and women to have to use the same public restrooms, you go right ahead and support it. The way I see it, you women just don't want to do housework anymore.

Joe's representation of Debra's argument is surely a perverted one. He has not only drawn an unwarranted inference from it, he has oversimplified it beyond recognition.

Attacking the Fallacy: It is not always possible to know if an opponent has deliberately distorted your argument or has simply failed to understand or interpret it in the way that was intended. Whichever happens to be the case, it might be helpful to recapitulate the basic outline of your argument, or better yet, ask your opponent to summarize it for you. If he or she is willing to do so, that will put you in a better position to correct any misinterpretation or misrepresentation and to add any important omission. If you have the opportunity, you should insist that a fruitful or constructive debate is not possible unless every attempt has been made to understand what is being said on both sides. If your opponent insists on continuing to distort your position, call attention to this and correct the distortion in each counterresponse. In no case should you debate the issue on the distorter's terms; that is, you should not allow yourself to be forced into defending a distorted expression of your position.

Attacking a Straw

Definition: This fallacy consists in attacking an opponent's position by focusing critical attention on some point less significant than the main point or basic thrust of the argument.

An attack against a "straw" has a number of different forms. It may be an attack against a support or premise that bears no significant weight in the argument or one that can be easily knocked away without any serious damage to the argument. Sometimes it is an attack on a misrepresentation, a caricature, or a highly oversimplified version of an argument. In this case, of course, what is being attacked is not the real argument or point of view at issue, so a successful attack upon it does not do any damage to the real argument. Another way of attacking a straw is to attack a minor or insignificant point that has no crucial relation to the main or basic point of the argument, for instance, the arguer's illustrations. In such cases, the basic argument remains intact, for even if the objection lodged against an illustration or minor point is sound, the objection is a trivial one.

Examples: "Yes, I've examined the case for Christianity, but I just can't accept it. I simply can't swallow that stuff about a man walking on water or turning water into wine. You and I both know that's empirically impossible." The speaker is surely attacking straws in picking on what are clearly some of the least significant features of the Christian perspective. Indeed, they would hardly even qualify as weak supports. A successful attack on these features, then, would have no significant negative effect upon the argument for the Christian Faith.

Example:
Dr. Gable: Walking is one of the best kinds of exercise you can get. One should always walk rather than ride whenever possible. For example, rather than drive over to the cafeteria to eat lunch, it would be more beneficial to your health to walk.
Mr. Gold: But, Doctor, I don't eat at the cafeteria.

Mr. Gold is here attacking an illustration that Dr. Gable used to make her point. The fact that the illustration does not fit in Mr. Gold's case is irrelevant to the basic thrust of the argument about the benefits of walking.

Example:
Ben: Professor Provost, I don't understand why you failed me in philosophy this term.

Professor Provost: I think I can explain that very well. As you know, you failed the first test I gave, you were caught cheating on the last test, and you neglected to turn in any of the written assignments I gave. Besides, I don't think you ever contributed *anything* to class discussion.

Ben: But Professor Provost, my doctor had given me strict orders to keep my talking to an absolute minimum. Early in the fall I discovered that I had some growths on my vocal chords, and the doctor said that the only way to get rid of them was to keep from using my voice for a period of several months.

Professor Provost: Oh, I didn't know about that. I can see now why you didn't speak up in class, and under the circumstances you could not have been expected to. How is your throat now?

Ben: Fine. But the important point is that you have admitted that your evaluation of my performance in your course was based on a false understanding, so I should not have failed the course. Right?

Wrong! Ben has successfully blunted only the weakest point in Professor Provost's argument for failing him—his contribution to class discussion.

Attacking the Fallacy: If a critic is to have any degree of success in effectively damaging an argument, he or she must attack the *strongest* supports for a claim. One way to effectively disarm an opponent who seizes on straws is to make it clear which are your strongest and which are your weakest reasons in support of your claim. If the arguer then chooses to attack one of your weaker supports, you will have already acknowledged that it is a weak support, so damage to *it* does not significantly affect the soundness of your argument.

If an opponent knocks down or refutes a misrepresentation of, or insignificant point in, your argument, do not hesitate to point out the fact that your basic argument is still unscathed and that you would be interested in hearing a response to *it*.

Red Herring

Definition: This fallacy consists in attempting to hide the weakness of a position by drawing attention away from the real issue to a side issue.

The strange name of this fallacy comes from fox hunting, where a herring, cooked to a brownish-red color, is dragged across the trail of the fox in order to pull the hunting dogs temporarily off the scent. In argument, it takes the form of consciously or unconsciously steering a debate away from one issue to a different, although perhaps related, issue in such a way as to make it appear that the related issue is relevant to the issue at hand.

A very common form of red herring is "empty consolation," which seeks to draw attention away from a complaint or criticism by claiming that the complainant should be satisfied with an undesirable situation simply because "things could be worse" or the situation of some other person or group is worse. Though it is true that "things" could almost always be worse than they are, that is not the issue, and drawing attention to such a notion is a way to avoid dealing with the initial criticism or complaint.

Example: Many of us have had the experience of complaining about the low or unfair wages we receive for our labors, only to be told by one of our parents: "Well, you *could* be making fifteen dollars a week as I did when I was your age." Such "consolation" usually sidetracks our complaint in spite of its irrelevance.

Example:

Senator Clark: Why are you not willing to support the antiabortion amendment? Don't you have any feelings at all for the unborn children whose lives are being indiscriminately blotted out?
Senator Davenport: I just don't understand why you people who get so worked up about the lives being blotted out by abortion don't have the same feelings about the thousands of lives that are blotted out every year by an indiscriminate use of handguns. Is not the issue of the sanctity of human life involved in both issues? Why have you not supported us in our efforts at gun-control legislation?

Senator Davenport's concern here is no doubt a very important one, but that concern is not related in any obvious way to the abortion issue or at least to the question of why she is not supporting the antiabortion amendment. The issue of gun control in this context is a red herring; that is, it inappropriately directs attention away from the primary issue at hand.

Example:

Dot: I'm convinced that your proposal to adopt an honor code here at our school just won't work. We don't have a tradition for it. Even institutions like West Point that have had a long history with an honor code are finding it no longer workable. Public school teachers, I understand, even refuse to listen to so-called tattletales. In fact, it is the tattletale who is now considered to be at fault if he or she informs the teacher about the behavior of another student.
Georgeanna: But don't you agree that the honor code has worked well in the past for those institutions that have used it? Can you deny that it has had a long and revered history at West Point and at other prestigious institutions?

The issue is not whether the honor code has worked well in the past in certain institutions. That is a red herring that is made to appear a relevant consideration in the discussion of the real issue, which is whether the honor code should now be initiated by an institution that has no tradition for it.

Attacking the Fallacy: To "hold the reins" on a heated argument or discussion is indeed not an easy task. Red herrings creep very subtly into the counterarguments of most all of us. Detecting when the focus of an argument has been maneuvered from the main to a side issue requires constant surveillance. Moreover, your frequent reminder of "that's not the issue" may not always be understood by your opponent. Therefore, you should be prepared to explain *how* the issue has been sidetracked or *why* a certain issue is appropriately classified as a red herring.

Resort to Humor or Ridicule

Definition: This fallacy consists in intruding humor or ridicule into an argument in an effort to cover up an inability or unwillingness to answer an opponent's position effectively. Humor is used as a substitute for relevant evidence.

Humor is one of the most effective diversionary tactics available, because a clever and well-delivered remark can blunt very quickly the force of an opponent's argumentative advantage in the minds of an audience, toward whom such humor is primarily directed. Moreover, it can quickly bring an audience over to one's own side, even though there is no logical justification for such a shift.

Appeal to humor can take a number of different forms. It might be a pun created from a remark in an opponent's proposal or argument, a not-so-serious response to a serious claim or question, a humorous anecdote, or just plain ridicule of an opponent's position or remarks. Ridicule of another person, of course, is an effective device only if it is not overly cruel; that is, it must be good humored enough to precipitate some spontaneous laughter. If it is too sharp, it might tend to weaken the position of the one who uses it by eliciting the audience's sympathy for the target.

Example: Suppose a philosophy student has just read through the first eight chapters of this book on fallacies and has begun to pay closer attention to the arguments of his professors and fellow students. Suppose, also, that he discovers in his political science class that Professor Stewart consistently commits the fallacy of contrary-to-fact hypothesis. He confronts the professor with this fact during the class discussion of a particular issue. Rather than examining the charge to determine if it is justifiable, Professor Stewart might blunt the force of the charge by saying: "Well, class, *Socrates* must have slipped into our class while we were not noticing. Now what did you say I did? Commit the fallacy of—what did you call it?—the contrary-to-fact hypothesis? I didn't know philosophers were concerned about *facts*." If this tactic were to work with his audience, the professor might be able to avoid facing squarely the charge against the soundness of his reasoning.

Example: Imagine the following conversation between a candidate for President of the United States on the Socialist ticket and a young reporter at a news conference:

Reporter: It seems to me that, if you were elected President, the Congress with which you would have to work would not be very cooperative at all. How could you, as President, bring about any reform or help enact any beneficial legislation with a Congress that was almost totally opposed to your programs?

Socialist candidate: Well, if I were elected, about half of the members of Congress would drop dead of heart attacks, and half of my problem would be solved from the outset.

The Socialist candidate is clearly attempting to dodge the reporter's question, although it seems to be one that deserves a serious response.

Attacking the Fallacy: If the humorous intrusion is a genuinely clever one, you could perhaps show appropriate appreciation of it, for sound argument need not be totally cheerless. A response in kind might even be an effective countermove on your part in order to regain your argumentative advantage or at least whatever position you previously had. However, at the appropriate moment, you should reiterate the basic claim at issue and insist upon a serious response.

Exercises

A. Identify the particular diversionary tactic in each of the following:

1. **Student:** The opinions of the students are completely ignored in the process of determining both curricular changes and social programs. The students should have a much greater voice in campus governance. We have a very great stake in this institution, and we think that we have a positive contribution to make.

   Professor: The faculty are the ones who need a greater voice. Professors can be fired without explanation, and they have no control over who is promoted or given tenure. Their opinions about budgetary allotments are completely ignored. Why aren't you concerned about the injustice being experienced by the faculty?

2. **Wife:** Rick, I'm tired of staying home every day, washing dishes, cleaning house, chasing the kids, and fixing meals. I would like to do something different with my life. I'd like to feel I was making some significant contribution. As it is, I feel worthless. How would you like to have to stay home and do the things I do every day—day after day?

   Husband: Look, Toni, into everyone's *wife* a little pain must fall.

3. **A:** It doesn't make much sense any more to prepare oneself for a specific vocation in college. In a technological age, change takes place so rapidly that job training usually becomes obso-

lete within ten years. I suggest that we maintain a strong non-vocationally oriented, liberal arts curriculum. That way our students will be prepared to go in a number of different vocational directions.

B: Do you really think that you could prove that a job-oriented technical education is obsolete in exactly ten years or less?

4. You shouldn't complain! You're *lucky* that women on this campus can stay out until 1 o'clock at night. Women here used to have to be in by 10 o'clock.

5. **A:** The installment method of buying has several advantages. It allows people with moderate incomes to have what they want—things they would have to go without if cash were required. It considerably expands the economy and raises the standard of living for millions of people. It even provides employment for many who are needed just to maintain records of installment accounts.

B: So? Even the "Mafia" provides gainful employment. But does that make the "Mafia" a good *idea*?

6. **Daughter:** If two people really love each other and have committed themselves to each other, I don't see any reason why they shouldn't live together. Phillip and I really do love each other, Mother. Someday we may get married, but right now we simply want to be close to each other.

Mother: The way I see it is that you're just looking for an excuse to go to bed together. Your whole attitude about this thing makes sex something cheap!

7. Two candidates for public office are debating in a public forum:

Candidate A: If I am elected, I promise to do everything I can to make our streets safe enough that our wives can walk the streets at night.

Candidate B: What is it you want to do—make hookers out of our wives?

8. **Parent A:** I think it would be a good idea for us to encourage the children to watch less television and get more physical exercise.

Parent B: You think I've let the kids become a bunch of lazy, unhealthy, television addicts, don't you?

9. **A:** I think the administration is entirely justified in dismissing Professor Van Zandt. He's never prepared for his lectures, he makes off-color remarks to his female students, he grades arbitrarily, and he isn't even friendly toward his students.

B: I disagree with you. He always says "hello" to me every time I see him.

10. I don't see why you are so concerned with the problem of alcoholism; the drug problem is in many respects no less an important national problem.

B. From among all the fallacies studied to this point, choose the fallacy that most closely resembles the problem exhibited in each of the following:

11. During a debate on the subject of biological evolution, the opponent of the evolutionary hypothesis confronts the proevolutionist: "Would you please tell us whether you more closely favor the apes on your father's side or on your mother's side of the family?"

12. The total number of students enrolled is steadily decreasing. The students are restless and unhappy, and many are threatening to transfer to some other college. It is my opinion that we had better revise our curriculum before it's too late.

13. I don't understand why I'm always sick. I eat a well-balanced meal three times a day. I have always been especially careful about eating the right foods and in the proper amounts, but still I seem to have something wrong with me most of the time.

14. A: Why are you so opposed to the singing of hymns in worship services?

B: Don't you know that many hymn tunes used to be drinking songs sung in taverns?

15. A: I bet you can't guess what kind of magazine I saw your father looking at down at the drug store.

B: What kind?

A: Well . . . maybe I'd better not say.

16. I think that we should adopt this new curricular proposal. After all, it has been unanimously endorsed by the college's Board of Trustees. The people who are entrusted with running the college should know what they're talking about when it comes to deciding the best curriculum for the school.

17. If the faculty and staff of this college are not willing to support my reelection to Congress, it may be a long time before you get that new exit that you've been wanting—one that leads directly from the Interstate to your campus. By the way, how much direct federal aid did your school receive last year?

18. Daughter: Father, I really don't think you understand my position concerning women's rights. What I am saying is that I think that a woman should not be discriminated against in any way. Any opportunity that is open to men should also be open to women.

Father: Oh, I think I understand! You think that it should be just as socially acceptable for women to "sleep around" as it is for men.

19. But, Cynthia, you *must* have a church wedding. No one in our family has ever been married outside the church. Your father and I, your grandparents, and your brothers and sisters have all been married in the church.

20. A: Why are you dropping out of your Latin class?

B: Well, I wasn't doing very well anyway, but the real reason is that I missed the mid-term examination. I was involved in a serious accident on my way to class the day of the exam. I wasn't hurt, but the other guy was banged-up pretty bad.

A: Can't you make up the test?

B: No, Professor Morris' policy states that there are no make-ups except in the case of a student's illness.

A: Don't you think that he would let you make it up under the circumstances? Why don't you ask him?

B: What's the use? He said that the only exception was a student's illness, and I wasn't sick!

IX
Statistical Fallacies

The fallacies discussed in this chapter are kinds of reasoning that make improper use of statistical data, especially those cases in which an arguer infers a conclusion on the basis of data too limited in quantity or data of an unrepresentative quality.[1] Other statistical fallacies include inferring a conclusion from data that are actually irrelevant to the claim at issue or from data whose accuracy is dubious at best. There is no attempt in this chapter to deal with many of the very complex problems related to statistical analysis. My much more limited purpose is to focus attention on some of the more common errors we commit when we draw conclusions from statistical data and to make some suggestions for dealing with such data in everyday situations.

Insufficient Sample

Definition: This fallacy consists in drawing an inductive generalization from too small a sample.

It is always a difficult problem to determine what constitutes a sufficient number of instances for drawing any particular inductive conclusion. An increase in the number of instances usually means that the claim for which those instances are evidence will be more sound, although there is probably a point beyond which the increase in the number of instances would have a negligible effect upon the soundness of a claim. There is a common tendency to draw a conclusion or

---

[1]An argument that involves either data of limited quantity or data of unrepresentative quality is sometimes referred to as a *hasty generalization.* However, I employ a distinct name for each of these cases as a means of identifying more precisely the problematic character of the argument.

generalization based upon only the few instances of a phenomenon that come to our attention. In fact, a generalization is often drawn from a single case. An argument form that requires statistical data can hardly qualify as a statistical argument if the data are constituted by only one or a few instances. Indeed, such reasoning is very often little more than an effort to justify a preconceived notion or point of view.

Example: I'm convinced that Vitamin C really works. Every member of my family used to have at least one good winter cold every year. Last fall each of us started taking 1,000 mg. of Vitamin C a day and there hasn't been even a sniffle at our house in over nine months." Such data may be interesting enough to encourage some people to consider a regular program of Vitamin C consumption, but it hardly makes the case for the effectiveness of the drug. A number of other reasons could possibly account as well or better for the no-cold phenomenon in a particular nine-month period. The speaker possibly has other evidence for the effectiveness of Vitamin C; however, that evidence is not provided as a part of the argument. On the basis of the evidence given, to conclude very much about the cold-preventing effects of Vitamin C would not be justified.

Example: A common experience is to stop by a grocery store where we don't normally shop to pick up a few items. If we discover that the price on several items is lower than the price on those items at the other store, we may infer that we should change grocery stores in order to cut down on our monthly grocery bill. However, such an inference would be unwarranted, for the sample used is too small. A more comprehensive comparative survey of the prices on the items we typically buy during the month might reveal that there would be very little difference between the total bills.

Example: "Because Tom's experience with his ex-wife was such a bad one, he has no intention of ever marrying again. In fact, he has even tried to talk me out of my marriage plans." Tom's reasoning is based on too small a sample. His one experience with marriage apparently convinced him that marriage was not a worthwhile institution for himself, his friends, and probably anyone else. However, it is quite possible that his one negative experience with marriage could be attributed to his mate rather than to the institution itself. It can at least be said that the question concerning the value of marriage deserves more critical analysis.

Attacking the Fallacy: Those who confront you with arguments based upon a single case or an insufficient sample are, unfortunately, usually convinced that they are offering a sound argument. Perhaps the reason that it seems so convincing to them is that it often involves or comes out of a significant personal experience. However, an existential insight falls far short of being a sound argument. It is possible, of course, that what appears to be a one-instance generalization, or what might be called the fallacy of the lonely fact, may not be intended as an argument at all; it may simply be a claim accompanied by an illustration. If such is the case, the arguer should make that clear, for evidence and illustrations perform very different functions. That distinction, however, is usually not clear. If you suspect that mere illustrations are being used as if they were evidence, an effective attack might go something like this: "That is an interesting illustration, but do you have any statistical *evidence* to support your claim?"

Unrepresentative Statistics

Definition: This fallacy consists in drawing an inductive generalization based upon unrepresentative data.

Qualitatively unrepresentative data may be not proportionately drawn from all relevant subclasses or may be atypical in some other way. If one wished to generalize about the opinion of the American people on a particular issue, it would be appropriate to consider data proportionately drawn from subclasses based on race, age, educational and professional status, sex, geographical area, and perhaps even religion. Other subclasses, such as body weight and hair color, would in most cases be irrelevant.

One kind of atypical data might be data of differing quality. If one compared statistics gathered with modern techniques of statistical reporting and analysis with statistics gathered under very different methodological and technical conditions, any conclusion would be highly questionable. For example, if one were to compare statistics on the number of violent crimes committed in the United States in 1978 with statistics on similar phenomena in 1940, the comparative conclusion would be suspect.

Example: It would be unwarranted to conclude that most children today are interested in music and dance merely because almost all the school-age children of the professors at King College take either violin, piano, horn, or ballet lessons. Such a small sample of children probably should not be considered as representative, nor should a college community be considered a typical community; hence, any conclusion based only on such data would be highly questionable.

Example: "We had a mock election on campus today, and the Democratic candidate won. So I am pretty confident that she will win the election in November, especially as over 2,000 students voted. That seems to be a big enough sample. Don't you agree?" A college population hardly qualifies as a representative sample of voters, even if the size of the sample is actually larger than the number usually polled by George Gallup and his associates. A sample must not only be large enough, it must also be genuinely random. If it is not drawn from relevant representative subclasses, the size of the sample is of no consequence.

Example: "It has been concluded from a recent study involving over 100,000 people in the state of Florida that 43 percent of the American people now spend at least two hours a day in some form of recreational activity." To draw such a conclusion about the leisure-time activities of the American people would not be warranted. The state of Florida is populated by a disproportionate number of retired and recreation-oriented people, so data based on a Florida population alone would be unrepresentative.

Attacking the Fallacy: If you have reason to believe that the arguer has not matched the sufficient quantity of his or her statistics with a sufficient quality, and perhaps has some difficulty in seeing the difference, you might use an absurd example in your attack. For example, if one were attempting to assess the potential market for a new dog food by determining the number of American households with one or more dogs, one would hardly get representative data if one interviewed only those attending dog shows. Such data might be quantitatively sufficient, but the proportion of people owning dogs would not be the same as the proportion of people owning dogs in the entire population.

If your opponent is not shaken by your charge that the particular statistics are unrepresentative, you might try to conceive of another set of unrepresentative data of the same size that could be used to support a claim that was contrary to the claim at issue. If samples of equal size could support two very different conclusions, it should be clear that there is something wrong with the quality of the sample.

Gambler's Fallacy

Definition: This fallacy consists in arguing that, because a chance event has had a certain run in the past, the probability of its occurrence in the future is significantly altered.

This is a fallacy that is typically committed by gamblers who are also losers. They are losers because they think that their chances of winning are better or significantly altered in their favor because of a certain run of events in the immediate past. Remember the loser who says, "I can't lose now, I'm hot," or the big loser who says, "My luck has got to change, I haven't had a single win all night. I'm betting everything on this one." Such people seem to be unaware that a chance event like the outcome of a coin toss or a roll of the dice is totally independent of all the tosses or rolls preceding it. To commit the gambler's fallacy, then, is to draw an inference principally on the assumption that the probability of a chance event's turning out in a particular way is affected by the series of similar chance events preceding it.

Even though this fallacy is common to the thinking of gamblers, it is not unique to them. Consider the parents who already have three sons and are quite satisfied with the size of their family. However, they both would really like to have a daughter. They commit the gambler's fallacy when they infer that their chances of having a girl are better because they have already had three boys. They are wrong. The sex of the fourth child is causally unrelated to any preceding chance event or series of such events. Their chances of having a daughter are no better than 1 in 2, that is, fifty-fifty.

Example: "Every time I open my mail it seems I get an offer of chances to win a lot of money or other prizes in some kind of drawing. Accompanying the chances to win there is always an opportunity to subscribe to magazines or to purchase products. Even though I never purchase anything, I usually mail back the coupon to see if I have won anything. I haven't won anything yet, but I figure my odds are getting better every time." As long as this person is not sending in more than one coupon for each contest, the chances of winning any particular contest do not improve.

Example: "It's been heads five times in a row. I'm sticking with tails." There is no more likelihood that the next toss of the coin will be tails than that it will be heads, in spite of the fact that most of us are inclined to believe that the odds would be in favor of its being tails.

Attacking the Fallacy: One of the best ways of attacking this fallacy is to show how such thinking could lead to contrary conclusions. Consider the once-a-month poker player who has had poor hands all evening. The longer this series of unfortunate events continues, the more such a player might be led to conclude that "this just isn't my night"; but one could just as well conclude that "surely my time is coming; I'm bound to get a good hand soon." Neither conclusion is warranted, because both derive from a misunderstanding of the character of chance events. Moreover, there is apparently no good reason why a person should draw one conclusion rather than its contrary. The choice appears to be almost wholly arbitrary. At best, it would depend upon what one's mood happened to be.

Fallacy of False Precision

Definition: This fallacy consists in making a claim with a kind of mathematical precision that is impossible to obtain.

It is not uncommon for an arguer to introduce statistical precision into a claim as a means of persuading a listener of the point at issue. A fallacy is committed when this precision is simply guessed at, when approximate data are treated as if they were precise, or when one uses data that cannot be known or obtained with the degree of precision claimed. It is commonly assumed, and perhaps correctly so, that the more precision one can introduce into one's claim, the more likely it is that a listener will regard it as true. For example, if your favorite television program has just been cancelled because, according to the network, not enough people were watching it, you might possibly be skeptical about such a claim. However, if the network claimed that in the last four weeks the highest proportion of the national viewing audience watching that program in any one week was 3.9 percent, you would be more likely to accept the claim as true and the cancellation as appropriate. The fact that statistical precision can have such effects is one of the reasons it is sometimes fabricated to strengthen a weak claim.

Probably no one of us is free from the tendency to introduce a false precision into even the most casual of our claims. For example, it is not unusual for a parent to say something like the following: "Three-fourths of the time, my children pay no attention to what I say." Such a claim is approximate at best, or nearly impossible to determine with the accuracy claimed. The purpose of expressing a claim with such alleged precision is probably to make the claim more pointed or dramatic. Nevertheless, when such unwarranted precision is introduced, for whatever reason, one still commits the fallacy of false precision. However, if nothing of substance is at stake, it can probably be safely ignored.

Example: Consider the claim that "one-third of all forest fires are intentionally set." It seems justifiable to assume that there is no way to obtain reliable data from which such a conclusion could be drawn, as the cause of many forest fires is unknown. Even if it were known that a fire started, for example, because of a cigarette, it would be virtually impossible to determine whether the cigarette was deliberately used to start the fire or whether it was the result of a careless toss into combustible material.

Example: One of the primary reasons cited for engaging in transcendental meditation (TM) is that "most of us use only 10 percent of our creative potential." Such a scientific-sounding claim has no doubt impressed many people with the possibilities open to them through TM of tapping the other 90 percent of their creative resources. However, one would have to know what constitutes 100 percent of one's creative potential in order to know what constitutes 10 percent of that potential, and it seems reasonable to assume that information about such a vaguely described possibility is not available or at least not precisely calculable. Nevertheless, many people would probably give much more credence to a claim stated with mathematical precision than they would to a more defensible (and nonfallacious) form of the same claim, for example, that "there is a lot of creative potential in each of us that we never use."

Example: The following is an excerpt from a letter sent to a former subscriber to *Intellectual Digest:*

> *By 1750, humanity's fund of knowledge had doubled from what it was at the birth of Christ. It doubled again by 1900. And again by 1950. And again by 1960. And again by 1968. Mankind is gaining knowledge at an astonishingly accelerating rate. Which means that it becomes increasingly difficult for any one individual to keep pace, and keep from becoming intellectually obsolete.*[2]

Such claims involve data that simply could not be obtained by any available means.

Attacking the Fallacy: The first step in confronting this fallacy is not to be intimidated or impressed by such tactics. Remember that if you give additional credence to a claim or assume it to be more accurate than it really could be, simply because it is expressed in precise mathematical language, you also are committing

---

[2]Quoted in Howard Kahane, *Logic and Philosophy*, 2nd ed. (Belmont, Calif.: Wadsworth Publishing Co., 1973), p. 245.

the fallacy of false precision. You might be tempted to counter an overly precise claim with a claim of your own that exhibits an even more absurd kind of precision, as an oblique method of exposing the questionable character of your opponent's claim. However, the counterclaim approach may be so oblique that your opponent might miss altogether what you are attempting to do, and your device would turn out to be simply diversionary. A better approach might be a direct one. For example, in response to the claim that "we use only 10 percent of our creative potential," you might ask several direct questions, such as: "How did you arrive at such a precise figure as 10 percent?" "Is it not the case that one must know what amount of creativity constitutes 100 percent in order to determine what 10 percent of such potential might be?" "Do you really mean 10 percent or is that just another way of saying that we use 'very little'?" This direct approach will at least force your opponent to respond seriously to your attack.

Exercises

A. Identify the statistical fallacy in each of the following:

1. If you ever ate in our cafeteria, you would see that institutional food is never very good.

2. During the American Revolution, 21 percent of the population supported the king, 23 percent supported the rebels, and the rest of the people really didn't care.

3. I think it's pretty safe to skip class today. Professor O'Neil wouldn't give us a pop quiz five days in a row. He's already given us one every day this week.

4. John Stuart Mill, a nineteenth-century English philosopher, was an extremely intelligent child who was taught most academic subjects at a very early age. He was able to read Latin poetry when he was only four years of age. If it had been possible to give him an I.Q. test, he would have had an I.Q. of at least 185.

5. All three sex offenders arrested this month by municipal police had previous records for the same crime. It seems that once a sex offender, always a sex offender.

6. Steve excuses his marrying again after his fifth divorce: "My luck is bound to change soon. Statistics show that at least half of American marriages are happy ones."

7. On the basis of a recent survey of a large number of representatively selected people in New York City, it has been discovered that less than 2 percent of the American people engage in hunting for sport.

8. I've seen several foreign-made films lately and I have found that foreign films deal with much more provocative themes and are much more artistically directed than American-made films.

9. Two hikers caught in a thunderstorm:
   A: What are we going to do? I'm scared to death of being struck by lightning. . . . Look! Lightning just hit that tree over there.
   B: Why don't we go stand under the tree that was just hit?

The probability of lightning's striking twice in exactly the same place is fantastically low. Surely we would be safe there.

10. I just don't believe those statistics about the number of major crimes in the United States sharply increasing over the past ten years. Here in Emory [a college town with a population of 323] we haven't had a single major crime committed in the last ten years.

B. From among all the fallacies studied to this point, choose the fallacy that most closely resembles the problem exhibited in each of the following:

11. A: I really like President Carter's basic domestic policy.
B: What's wrong with his *foreign* policy?

12. I'm surprised to learn that you like Nietzsche's philosophy. You know that Hitler was a great admirer of Nietzsche, don't you?

13. A: What can you do with a major in philosophy? Does it prepare you for any job?
B: No.
A: Then what good does it do to major in it?

14. If you reject the miracles of Jesus in the New Testament, the next thing you know, you'll be rejecting the virgin birth, then the resurrection, and then the whole idea of incarnation. In other words, you'll end up saying that Jesus was just a man—not divine at all—and that will lead you to question the very Scriptures themselves. And if you can't believe the Scriptures, you can't even believe in God.

15. I just don't understand how Senator Foster got elected. I've talked with the people at the office, with those in my Sunday School class, and with my friends at the country club, and I haven't found a single person who voted for him.

16. Neither the textbooks nor the teachers in our public schools are as good as they used to be. This was confirmed by a recent CBS survey of parents of American school children. Over 63 percent of them say that our teachers and texts are worse than when they were students.

17. Henry Kissinger, Secretary of State under both President Nixon and President Ford, said in a recent interview in *U.S. News & World Report* that historians will probably describe Presidents Nixon and Ford as having developed very strong, forward-looking, and well-defined foreign policies.

18. During the discussion on an important issue in a faculty meeting, one professor says to another: "Your criticisms of this proposal are simply delaying tactics. Everything you've said this morning is simply an attempt to camouflage your own negativism. I regard your whole attitude as basically deceitful and unprofessional."

19. One legislator to another: "Henry, you of all people should be interested in the passage of the Equal Rights Amendment. If it passes in our state and becomes a part of the Constitution, you could then file a new child custody suit, on grounds of sexual discrimination, and at least have a better chance of getting custody of your kids."

20. The reason that many people read Saul Bellow's books is that he is a famous author.

X
Fallacies of Deductive Inference

The fallacies discussed in this chapter are usually described as formal fallacies, in that they improperly infer a conclusion by means of an invalid argument form or procedure; that is, they violate a particular rule of valid deductive logic. Some attention will be given to the rules violated by these fallacies, but no attempt is made to deal with the more complex problems of formal logic. Moreover, only the most commonly encountered deductive fallacies will be treated.

Fallacies of Syllogistic Reasoning

Some of the most common formal fallacies are the fallacies encountered in categorical syllogisms. A standard categorical syllogism is an argument comprised of three categorical statements or propositions. A categorical statement consists of only two terms and asserts that either all or some members of the class of things referred to in the subject term are either included or excluded from the class of things referred to in the predicate term. Two of these statements are premises, and the other is the conclusion.

Each statement is either an A, E, I, or O type of proposition. The four capital letters used to designate these statements come from the first two vowels in the Latin word *affirmo*, which means "I affirm," and the first two vowels in the Latin word *nego*, which means "I deny." Thus, A and I statements are affirmative statements, and E and O statements are negative statements. An A statement is a *universal* affirmative statement, as in "All Democrats are liberals," and an E statement is a *universal* negative statement, as in "No Democrats are liberals." The sign of a universal proposition is the word *all* or *no*. An I statement is a *particular* affirmative statement, as in "Some Democrats are liberals," and an O statement is a *particular* negative statement, as in "Some Democrats are not liberals." The sign of a particular proposition is the word *some*.

In a properly formed categorical syllogism, there are three and only three terms, each of which appears two and only two times in the argument. One of the terms, the *middle* term, appears in both premises but not in the conclusion. The other two terms are called *end terms*. The term that appears as the predicate term in the conclusion is referred to as the *major term*. The term that appears as the subject term in the conclusion is referred to as the *minor term*. The premise in which the predicate or major term appears is called the *major premise;* the premise in which the subject or minor term appears is called the *minor premise*. The following argument is an example of a well-formed syllogism:

All Democrats are liberals. (major premise)

No antiabortionists are liberals. (minor premise)

No antiabortionists are Democrats. (conclusion)

This syllogism has the requisite three and only three terms. The middle term, *liberals*, appears twice and only twice in the premises. The end terms, *antiabortionists* and *Democrats*, also appear twice and only twice. The major term (predicate term of the conclusion) is *Democrats*, and the minor term (subject term of the conclusion) is *antiabortionists*. The first premise is an A statement, and both the second premise and the conclusion are E statements. This syllogism also satisfies the rules for a valid syllogism, which means that it does not commit any formal or deductive fallacy.

There are at least three rules for a valid syllogism, and the violation of any one of them is sufficient to render a syllogism invalid.[1] *First, the middle term must be distributed at least once. Second, an end term that is distributed in the conclusion must also be distributed in one of the premises. Third, the number of negative premises must equal the number of negative conclusions.*[2] This last rule obviously excludes the possibility of two negative premises.

In order to understand and apply the rules of a valid syllogism, one must first become acquainted with the notion of distribution. A term is called *distributed* if the statement in which the term occurs makes a claim about every member of the class designated by that term. For example, in the universal affirmative or A statement "All Democrats are liberals," something is being claimed about every member of the class of Democrats, although no claim is being made about every member of the class of liberals. Hence, in an A statement, the subject term is a distributed term

---

[1]The rationale for these rules can be demonstrated by means of so-called Venn diagrams, which employ circles to represent the logical relations between the terms in the premises of a syllogism. One may find this diagrammatic analysis and also a fuller discussion of the rationale for these rules in almost any standard textbook on deductive logic.

[2]This third rule is rarely violated by a syllogistic argument that·does not at the same time violate at least one of the other two rules. Moreover, when an argument violates this third rule, its invalidity is almost impossible to conceal; that is, it has very little deceptive character. Hence, the so-called fallacy of unequal negation is neither a common nor an important enough error to warrant special treatment in this study.

and the predicate term is an undistributed one. In the universal negative or E statement "No Democrats are liberals," a claim is made about every Democrat *and* every liberal, namely, that every Democrat is a nonliberal and that every liberal is excluded from the class of Democrats. Hence, both the subject *and* the predicate terms are distributed in an E statement. In the case of the particular affirmative or I statement "Some Democrats are liberals," no claim is made about every Democrat, and no claim is made about every liberal. In an I statement, then, neither the subject nor the predicate term is distributed. In the particular negative or O statement "Some Democrats are not liberals," no claim is made about every Democrat, although a claim *is* made about every liberal, namely, that every member of the class of liberals will exclude at least those particular Democrats referred to in the subject term of the statement. Hence, only the predicate term is distributed in an O statement.

In order to determine whether a fallacy of syllogistic reasoning has been committed, it is important to know exactly which terms are distributed and which are not distributed. A brief summary of the facts of distribution is as follows: The subject term of a universal statement (A and E) is always distributed; the predicate term of a negative statement (E and O) is always distributed; all other terms are always undistributed. A mnemonic device suggested by one writer that may help you to remember the facts of distribution is AsEbInOp.[3] This word suggests that in an A statement the subject (s) is distributed, in an E statement both (b) the subject and the predicate are distributed, in an I statement neither (n) the subject nor the predicate is distributed, and in an O statement only the predicate (p) term is distributed.

One other matter to which attention should be drawn is the problem of translating the premises and conclusions of syllogistic arguments into standard form. To be in standard form, each of the three statements must be formulated into an A, E, I, or O statement. For example, the statement "Most of the Democrats that I know are not liberal at all" should be translated as an O statement, namely, "Some Democrats are not liberals." In this statement, as in all I and O statements, *some* refers to any number that is at least one and is less than all. The standard form for a statement that makes an individual or *singular* claim is a universal (A or E) statement. For example, the claim "John is a Democrat" should be translated into an A statement, namely, "All people identical with John are people who are Democrats." The standard way of translating a statement containing the word *only*, as in the claim "Only liberals are Democrats," is to eliminate the *only* and exchange the positions of the subject and the predicate terms so that it reads as an A statement, namely, "All Democrats are liberals."

If a claim is stated in a conditional form, it should be translated as a universal statement. For example, the claim "If one is a Democrat, then he or she is a liberal" should be translated as an A statement, namely, "All democrats are liberals." If the consequent phrase is negated, as in "If one is a Democrat, then he or she is not a liberal," it should be translated as an E statement, namely, "No Democrats are liberals." In other words, when a conditional statement is translated, the

[3]Stephen Barker, *The Elements of Logic* (New York: McGraw-Hill Book Company, 1965), p. 46.

antecedent (the *if* phrase) becomes the subject term of a universal statement, and the consequent (the *then* phrase) becomes the predicate term. If the word *unless* is used to introduce a conditional phrase, it should be translated as *if not.* For example, the statement "Unless Bruce is sick, he will be at work tomorrow" should be translated as "If Bruce is not sick, he will be at work tomorrow." It can then be translated as an A statement, namely, "All people identical with a nonsick Bruce are people who will be at work tomorrow."

The presence of an *only if* in a conditional statement requires an additional operation. For example, the claim that "John is a Democrat only if he is a liberal" should first be translated into a standard conditional form, namely, "If John is a Democrat, he is a liberal." In such translations the *only* is eliminated and the *if* is moved to introduce the opposite phrase. The resultant conditional statement can then be easily translated into a universal statement, namely, "All people identical with a Democratic John are people who are liberals."

A very useful device for translating some statements into standard form is the so-called "Square of Opposition," an abbreviated version of which is illustrated below.

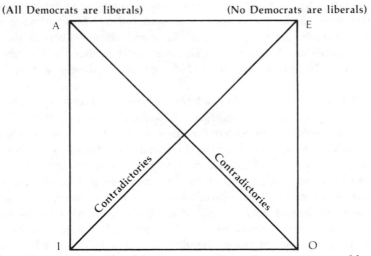

(All Democrats are liberals)   (No Democrats are liberals)

(Some Democrats are liberals)   (Some Democrats are not liberals)

As illustrated, A and O statements contradict each other. Hence, the claim that "It is *not* the case that some Democrats are not liberals" (not O) is equivalent to "All Democrats are liberals" (A). Likewise, a *negated* A statement is equivalent to an O statement. Moreover, E and I statements contradict each other. Hence, the claim that "It is *not* true that no Democrats are liberals" (not E) is equivalent to "Some Democrats are liberals" (I). Likewise, a *negated* I statement is equivalent to an E statement.

One other problem of translation that may be encountered is created by a term's appearing in one part of an argument in a negative form and in another part of that argument in an affirmative form, thus causing the argument to have, in effect, more than three terms. As a standard syllogism must have three and only three terms, if a term appears in two forms, they must be "lined-up" so that either both forms of the term are negative or both forms are affirmative. There are three translation procedures that help bring this about: obversion, conversion, and contraposition. In order to *obvert* a statement, one first changes the quality of the claim to its opposite; that is, one changes it from affirmative to negative (A becomes E or I becomes O) or from negative to affirmative (E becomes A or O becomes I). Second, one negates the predicate term. For example, the obverse of the claim that "No Democrats are nonliberals" (E) is the claim that "All Democrats are liberals" (A). Similarly, the claim that "Some Democrats are liberals" (I) is the obverse of "Some Democrats are not nonliberals" (O). In each of these cases the quality of the statement has been changed, and the predicate term has been negated. Nevertheless, the original statement and its obverse are equivalent statements.

In some cases it might be desirable to *convert* the subject and predicate terms before performing the operation of obversion, so that the term one wishes to negate in the obversion procedure will be in the predicate position. Conversion, which is simply the exchange of the subject and predicate terms, is always possible with E and I statements. For example, the claim that "No Democrats are liberals" means the same thing as "No liberals are Democrats," and the claim that "Some Democrats are liberals" means the same thing as "Some liberals are Democrats." Conversion, however, is *not* possible with A and O statements, as the distribution of the terms in these statements is uneven.

It is possible, however, to *contrapose* A and O statements. In contraposition, the subject and predicate terms are exchanged, and both are then negated. For example, the contrapositive of the A statement "All nonliberals are non-Democrats" is "All Democrats are liberals." A conditional statement may be contraposed by exchanging the antecedent and the consequent and negating both. For example, the contrapositive of "If Bruce is a Democrat, he is a liberal" would be "If Bruce is not a liberal, he is not a Democrat." The procedure of contraposition is rarely required and is applicable only to A and O statements.

If one has translated a syllogistic argument into a standard form, it is then ready to be tested for its validity. A simple method for determining whether a particular syllogistic argument satisfies the rules of a valid syllogism involves three steps: First, symbolize the middle and the two end terms in the syllogism by the first letter of a key word in each. Second, identify each premise and the conclusion as an A, E, I, or O statement. If one follows these first two steps for the example used earlier, the result would be as follows:

D (A) L (All Democrats are liberals.)

A (E) L (No antiabortionists are liberals.)

A (E) D (No antiabortionists are Democrats.)

In this example, D = Democrats, A = antiabortionists, and L = liberals. The letters (A), (E), and (E) simply identify the kinds of statements involved in the syllogism and are helpful in applying the rules of a valid syllogism.

The third step in testing the validity of a syllogism is to apply the three stated rules of validity, that is to check the argument for the appropriate distribution of terms and for evenness of negation. In the example above, the middle term (L) is distributed in the second premise. Hence, it satisfies the first rule. No end term (D or A) is distributed in the conclusion that is not also distributed in one of the premises. Therefore, the second rule is satisfied. There is also no uneven negation, for the conclusion is negative and there is exactly one negative premise. Therefore, because this argument satisfies all three rules, it should be regarded as valid.

Undistributed Middle Term

Definition: This fallacy of syllogistic reasoning consists in inferring a conclusion from two premises in which the middle term is not distributed.

This fallacy is a violation of one of the rules of a valid syllogism, namely, that the middle term must be distributed at least once. In other words, in at least one of the premises, some claim must be made about every member of the class designated by the middle term.

Example: "It is mostly the unhappy people in this world who commit suicide, and as we know that some rich people have killed themselves, we must conclude that at least some rich people are unhappy in spite of their wealth." If U = unhappy people, C = commit suicide, and R = rich people, this argument can be put into the following standard form:

U (I) C

R (I) C

R (I) U

Because the middle term (C) is the predicate term of a particular affirmative or I statement in both premises, it is not distributed in either premise. Therefore, the syllogism commits the fallacy of an undistributed middle term. The conclusion may be true, but the premises given do not warrant such a conclusion.

Example: "Some of your friends must be communists, for they are always criticizing the free enterprise system. That's the kind of criticism that communists consistently make." If F = friends, A = people who always criticize the free enterprise system, and C = communists, the form of this argument would look like this:

F (I) A

C (A) A

F (I) C

The middle term (A) is undistributed in both the major and the minor premises, as it is the predicate term in a particular affirmative or I statement and in a universal affirmative or A statement.

Example: "A well-written drama does not need elaborate scenery in order to be dramatically effective. I notice that the play that Edwards is producing does not require elaborate scenery. I assume, then, that it must be quite a well-written one." If W = well-written drama, R = dramas that do not require elaborate scenery to be dramatically effective, and P = play Edwards is producing, then the standard form of this syllogism is as follows:

W (A) R

P (I) R

_____

P (I) W

The second premise is categorized here as a particular affirmative or I statement, which can be rephrased as "Some plays (at least the one Edwards is producing) do not require elaborate scenery." That same premise, however, could also be categorized as a universal affirmative or A statement, which would read somewhat differently: "All plays identical with the one Edwards is producing do not require elaborate scenery." Nevertheless, in either case, the middle term (R) is undistributed, because it is the predicate of an affirmative statement.

Attacking the Fallacy: It is likely that many of the people who deserve to be confronted by their fallacious syllogistic reasoning will be unacquainted with either the notion of distribution or the rules of a valid syllogism. Moreover, some have argued that even the one who attacks such reasoning does not necessarily have to be acquainted with such technical matters. Indeed, it is said, one who senses "something wrong" with a syllogistic argument could simply construct a clever absurd example and expose the fallacy. It is my judgment, however, that unless one is acquainted with the notion of distribution and the rules of a valid syllogism, one could never be certain that a fallacy has or has not been committed. The absurd example method is, to be sure, a most effective method of demonstrating the fallaciousness of an argument; but an understanding of the mechanics of syllogistic reasoning would facilitate a wiser and more confident use of that method. Therefore, after you have ascertained by means of the rules of the syllogism that a syllogistic fallacy has definitely been committed, you could simply confront the arguer with an example of a syllogism that has true premises and an obviously absurd conclusion but that follows the same pattern of reasoning exhibited in the fallacious argument. Take, for example, the second illustration above, where the argument claims that "some of your friends are communists." If S, P, and M are substituted for the subject, predicate, and middle terms, respectively, the "friends" argument would exhibit the following pattern:

S (I) M

P (A) M

_____

S (I) P

A consistent substitution of terms in another argument following the same pattern of reasoning could produce an argument with true premises but with an obviously false or absurd conclusion: "If some horses (S) have teeth (M), and all cows (P) have teeth (M), then some horses (S) are cows (P)." Such an example would demonstrate clearly to the arguer the fallaciousness of this pattern of reasoning, as an argument with true premises and a false conclusion cannot be valid.

Illicit Distribution of an End Term

Definition: This fallacy of syllogistic reasoning consists in drawing a conclusion that includes a distributed end term that is not distributed in one of the premises.

The rule violated is that an end term that is distributed in the conclusion must be distributed in one of the premises. If the major or predicate term is illegitimately distributed in the conclusion, the error is often referred to as the fallacy of the illicit major; if the minor or subject term is causing the problem, it is referred to as the fallacy of the illicit minor.

Example: "Those parents who provide a solid foundation for ethical behavior give their children a genuinely sound moral education. Because religion provides such a foundation for morality, those parents who wish to give their children sound moral training should ground it in religion." If P = those who provide a foundation for ethical behavior, S = those who give their children a sound moral education, and R = religion, the standard form of this argument would look like this:

R (A) P

P (A) S

S (A) R

The minor or subject term (S) of the conclusion is a distributed one, although it is not distributed in the minor premise, where it is the predicate term of a universal affirmative or A statement. The argument therefore commits the fallacy of illicit distribution of the minor term.

Example: "Anybody who ignores the relevant facts in a situation is very likely to come to a false conclusion about it. The jury in a criminal trial is not likely to come to a false judgment, because it takes all relevant facts into account when making a decision." If I = people who ignore the relevant facts in a situation, F = people who come to a false conclusion, and J = jury, this argument in a standard form would read like this:

I (A) F

J (E) I

J (E) F

The major term (F) is distributed in the conclusion, but it is not distributed in the major premise, where it is the predicate of a universal affirmative statement. Hence, the conclusion illegitimately distributes the major term.

Example: "Everything that is morally right is just, but some actions that are in the best interests of all people are not really just. Hence, some morally right actions are not in the best interests of all people." If M = morally right actions, J = just actions, and B = actions in the best interests of all people, this argument might be set forth in the following manner:

> B (O) J
>
> M (A) J
> _____
>
> M (O) B

The major term (B) is distributed in the conclusion, but it is not distributed in the major premise, where it is the subject of a particular negative statement. Hence the argument exhibits an illicit distribution of the major term.

Attacking the Fallacy: An argument that exhibits the fallacy of illicit distribution of an end term may be attacked by the same method suggested for the fallacy of the undistributed middle term. Let us take the form of the "jury" argument above and express it in neutral symbolism:

> M (A) P
>
> S (E) M
> _____
>
> S (E) P

A consistent substitution of terms in another argument following the same pattern of reasoning could produce an argument with true premises but with an obviously false or absurd conclusion: "If all male students on campus (M) sometimes wear jeans (P), and no female students (S) are male students (M), then no female students (S) are people who wear jeans (P)." This pattern of reasoning cannot be valid, for a valid argument has a form such that, if the premises are true, the conclusion cannot be false; and the conclusion in this case is obviously false.

False Conversion

Definition: This fallacy consists in exchanging the subject and predicate terms in a universal affirmative or a particular negative statement or in reversing the antecedent and the consequent of a conditional statement and then inferring that such converted statements retain their original truth values.

The reason that A and O statements cannot be converted is that there is an uneven distribution of the two terms in each statement; that is, only one of the terms in each statement is distributed. In contrast, the distribution of terms in both the E and the I statement is even. Both of the terms in an E statement are distributed, and both of the terms in an I statement are undistributed. Thus, conversion is permissible in the case of E and I statements.

The reason that the antecedent and the consequent in a conditional statement cannot be reversed is that a sufficient condition, which is the antecedent in a conditional statement, does not function in the same way as a necessary condition, which is the consequent in a conditional statement.[4]

Example: From the truth of the claim that religious people are people who rely upon a power outside themselves, it could not be inferred that people who rely upon a power outside themselves are religious. An A statement, in this case "All religious people are those who rely upon a power outside themselves," cannot be converted and retain its original truth value. The fact that the converse of the A statement is not necessarily true could be demonstrated by pointing out that it is quite possible that a person could rely upon something outside himself or herself, for example, a parent, and not be religious at all.

Example: If it is true that all heroin addicts started by smoking marijuana, it cannot be inferred that the converse is true, that is, that marijuana smokers are or will become heroin addicts. The converted statement is a very different claim whose truth must be independently established.

Example: Suppose that Leigh says to her friend, "If you love me, you will do what I ask you to do." Suppose also that this conditional claim is true—that is, if the friend really does love Leigh, he will indeed do as she asks. However, one could not infer from the truth of that claim that the converse is true; that is, one could not conclude that if the friend does what he is asked to do, then that would be proof that he loves Leigh. Loving Leigh may be a sufficient condition for doing what she asks, but if the friend simply does what Leigh asks him to do, that would not be a sufficient condition for concluding that he loves her.

Attacking the Fallacy: An absurd example should convince your opponent that conversions of A and O statements are illegitimate. From "all chemists are scientists," one could obviously not conclude that "all scientists are chemists"; and from "some scientists are not chemists" one could obviously not conclude that "some chemists are not scientists." To attack the conversion of a conditional statement, you might use the following example to demonstrate its faulty character: If someone is the President of the United States, that person must be thirty-five years or older and a natural-born citizen; yet obviously if one is thirty-five years or older and a natural-born citizen, one is not necessarily the President of the United States.

Fallacies of Hypothetical Reasoning

Two of the most common formal fallacies are those found in conditional or hypothetical arguments. These fallacies misapply valid procedures of argument

[4]See p. 65.

involving the use of conditional statements. One valid form of conditional argument is called *affirming the antecedent* or *modus ponens*. It takes the following form:

If A, then B

A

Therefore, B

If we can assume that the first or hypothetical premise is true, then in all cases in which the antecedent (A) is true, the consequent (B) must be true. In other words, given the truth of the conditional premise, the affirmation of the antecedent requires the affirmation of the consequent.

Another valid form of conditional argument is called *denying the consequent* or *modus tollens*.[5] The form of this argument is as follows:

If A, then B

Not B

Therefore, not A

If we assume that the first or hypothetical premise is true, then in all cases in which the consequent (B) is false, the antecedent (A) must be false also. In other words, given the truth of the conditional premise, the denial of the consequent requires the denial of the antecedent.

There are two common forms of invalid conditional argument. These are called *affirming the consequent* and *denying the antecedent*. Each of these is often confused with one of the valid patterns. A mnemonic device that might be helpful in remembering these invalid patterns is *acda*, which is constituted by the initial letters of the names of the two invalid forms.

Denying the Antecedent

Definition: This fallacy consists in denying the antecedent of a conditional statement and then inferring the denial of the consequent.

This pattern of reasoning conforms to neither one of the valid forms of conditional argument. This invalid form is symbolized in the following manner:

If A, then B

Not A

Therefore, not B

However, from the denial of the antecedent no conclusion can be legitimately inferred.

Example: "If capital punishment actually deterred people from committing capital crimes, then it would be justified. But as it does not have that deterrent

[5]*Modus tollens* is an abbreviation for the Latin *modus tollendo tollens*, which means "the mood that denies by denying." *Modus ponens* is an abbreviation for the Latin *modus ponendo ponens*, which means "the mood that affirms by affirming."

effect, it is not a justifiable practice." There may be factors other than deterrence that are sufficient to justify capital punishment. Hence, the denial of the antecedent does not require the denial of the consequent.

Example: "Professor O'Neil told us that we would pass the course if we could correctly identify the fallacy example that he had put on the chalkboard. So I guess I failed the course; I couldn't identify it." If the antecedent is *not* true; that is, if one does not or cannot identify the fallacy, that does not entail that one will *not* pass the course. Professor O'Neil did not say that one would *not* pass the course if one could *not* identify the fallacy.

Attacking the Fallacy: An absurd example should clearly demonstrate the fallacious reasoning exhibited in an argument that denies the antecedent:

If Boots is a dog (A), then Boots is an animal (B).

Boots is not a dog (Not A).

Therefore, Boots is not an animal (Not B).

If Boots is a cat, a false conclusion has been inferred from true premises, which would be impossible if the argument form were a valid one.

Affirming the Consequent

Definition: This fallacy consists in affirming the consequent of a conditional statement and then inferring the antecedent.

This pattern of reasoning conforms to neither one of the valid forms of a conditional argument. This invalid form may be symbolized in the following way:

If A, then B

B

Therefore, A

From the affirmation of the consequent, however, no conclusion can be legitimately inferred.

Example: "If a deductive argument is sound, then it must be valid. There is no doubt that Phillip's argument is valid. Therefore, it must be a sound one." Not necessarily. Validity is a necessary condition of soundness; but a sufficient condition for a deductive argument's soundness is that it have both a valid form and true premises.

Example: "If the light comes on, the light bulb must be a good one. The bulb is a good one; I checked it myself this morning. Therefore, the light will come on." The light bulb's being good is only a necessary condition of the light's coming on; it is not a sufficient condition for that event. There are a number of other conditions that would have to be present in order for the light to come on.

Attacking the Fallacy: It has been suggested repeatedly that the absurd example method is a good method of exposing fallacious reasoning. To confront the fallacy of affirming the consequent, you might try this example:

> If you read this book (A), you will be able to recognize and successfully attack fallacious reasoning when you hear or read it (B).
>
> You are able to recognize and successfully attack fallacious reasoning when you hear or read it (B).
>
> ———————————————————————————————
>
> Hence, you must have read this book (A).

Although you may indeed have read this book, the fact that you are able to recognize and successfully attack fallacious reasoning in no way entails or requires that you must have read this book.

Exercises

A. Identify the fallacy of deductive inference in each of the following:

1. Newly constructed houses are very expensive, but the new houses are also very efficiently planned houses; so if you want an efficiently planned house, you are going to have to pay plenty for it.

2. Picasso's "Guernica" has artistic merit only if it is appreciated by most people, and it is. Hence, I think we can conclude that it does have artistic merit.

3. We know that the earth is spherically shaped, because spheres always cast curved shadows and we have found that the earth casts a curved shadow on the moon during a lunar eclipse.

4. Because none of our good teachers here is tenured and because our tenured faculty members are all very conservative, we at least know that none of our better teachers follows a conservative line.

5. People who obey the law will stay out of trouble with the police. Therefore, it could be concluded that those who have managed to stay out of trouble are those who don't go around breaking the law.

6. If Congress had strong, vigorous leadership, it would be able to override the President's veto on this strip-mining bill. However, because the Congressional leadership has not exhibited any strength whatsoever, the will of the President will prevail.

7. Because it is not the case that no acts of civil disobedience are nonviolent and because most morally justified acts are nonviolent acts, at least some acts of civil disobedience are justified from the moral point of view.

8. A: If my mother saw me go into this X-rated movie, I'd really be embarrassed.

B: Well, obviously your mother is *not* going to see you. You told me that she was out of town for the weekend. So there's no reason for you to be embarrassed.

9. Denise must not be home; she said that if the light was on when we came by, we could be assured that she had arrived home safely, and the light is not on.

10. If a person is given a proper upbringing by one's parents, he or she will treat others with respect. So if a person treats others with respect, we must conclude that he or she has indeed been given a proper upbringing.

B. From among all the fallacies studied to this point, choose the fallacy that most closely resembles the problem exhibited in each of the following:

11. Cynthia told me that if she failed Philosophy 101, she would drop out of school. As she has left school, I assume that she failed the course.

12. Husband to wife at supermarket: "Why are you getting such a small box of soap powder? As much of this stuff as we use, we could surely save a lot of money if we bought this Giant Economy Size."

13. All Christians love and care for other people. Therefore, people who love and care for others must be Christians, regardless of whether they refer to themselves by such a term.

14. A: It's absurd to say that we have any moral obligation at all toward any animal. For instance, I certainly don't feel any moral guilt in killing insects, mice, rats, or snakes.
B: Am I to understand that you wouldn't think a person morally blameworthy if he or she tried to drown little baby kittens or poured gasoline on a little dog, set fire to it, and watched it go crazy with pain?

15. If you are really interested in acquiring the ability to reason correctly, you should study logic. If you are serious about studying logic, you will surely read this book. Therefore, the people who read this book are people who are genuinely interested in learning sound reasoning.

16. As long as the United States keeps strong militarily, we can avoid involvement in any major war. We haven't been involved in a major war for over three decades. That must mean that we are strong militarily.

17. I have difficulty accepting the notion that all human events are the inevitable results of antecedent conditions, but I also have difficulty with the view that human beings can act apart from antecedent conditions. In other words, I find both determinism and indeterminism untenable. Surely the most defensible view lies somewhere between those extremes.

18. All 18-year-olds are eligible to vote. Of course, not all people who are eligible to vote take advantage of it. Hence there must be some 18-year-olds who do not exercise their rights.

19. The F.B.I. reports concerning the number of major crimes committed in the United States are quite deficient in at least one area—the number of rapes —because 70 percent of the victims of rape never report such crimes to the authorities.

20. Do you really expect me to *dignify* your questions about my proposal by answering them? They simply confirm what I've always thought about you anyway. Your thinking is shallow, naive, and uninformed. And I feel that you're wasting my time.

Answers to Exercises

Chapter I: 1. Misuse of vague expressions. **2.** False ambiguity. **3.** Syntactical ambiguity. **4.** Semantical ambiguity. **5.** Misuse of vague expressions. **6.** Semantical ambiguity. **7.** Equivocation. **8.** Illicit contrast. **9.** Fallacy of accent. **10.** Equivocation. **11.** Fallacy of accent. **12.** Distinction without a difference. **13.** Syntactical ambiguity. **14.** Argument by innuendo. **15.** Semantical ambiguity. **16.** False ambiguity. **17.** Equivocation. **18.** Distinction without a difference. **19.** Illicit contrast. **20.** Argument by innuendo.

Chapter II: 1. Loaded or complex question. **2.** Question-begging definition. **3.** Leading question. **4.** Circular reasoning. **5.** Apriorism. **6.** Question-begging expression. **7.** Circular reasoning. **8.** Apriorism. **9.** Question-begging definition. **10.** Leading question. **11.** Apriorism. **12.** Question-begging expression. **13.** Argument by innuendo. **14.** Loaded or complex question. **15.** Question-begging definition. **16.** Loaded or complex question. **17.** Question-begging expression. **18.** Distinction without a difference. **19.** Syntactical ambiguity. **20.** Fallacy of accent.

Chapter III: 1. Faulty analogy. **2.** Misuse of a generalization. **3.** Fallacy of novelty. **4.** Fallacy of composition. **5.** Fallacy of the continuum. **6.** Fallacy of division. **7.** False alternatives. **8.** Is-ought fallacy. **9.** Wishful thinking. **10.** Fallacy of the continuum. **11.** Fallacy of the golden mean. **12.** Fallacy of composition. **13.** Fallacy of division. **14.** Faulty analogy. **15.** Fallacy of the continuum. **16.** Leading question. **17.** False alternatives. **18.** Circular reasoning. **19.** Misuse of vague expressions. **20.** Wishful thinking.

Chapter IV: 1. Contrary-to-fact hypothesis. **2.** Fallacy of negative proof. **3.** Inference from a label. **4.** Unsuitable use of a cliché. **5.** Neglect of relevant evidence. **6.** Contrary-to-fact hypothesis. **7.** Unsuitable use of a cliché. **8.** Fallacy of negative proof. **9.** Neglect of relevant evidence. **10.** Inference from a label. **11.** Fallacy of negative proof. **12.** Contrary-to-fact hypothesis. **13.** False ambiguity. **14.** Misuse of a generalization. **15.** Neglect of relevant evidence. **16.** Fallacy of novelty. **17.** Fallacy of negative proof. **18.** Is-ought fallacy. **19.** Fallacy of the golden mean. **20.** Unsuitable use of a cliché.

Chapter V: 1. Causal oversimplification. **2.** *Post hoc* fallacy. **3.** Confusion of a necessary with a sufficient condition. **4.** Domino fallacy. **5.** *Post hoc* fallacy. **6.** Neglect of a common cause. **7.** Confusion of cause and effect. **8.** Confusion of a necessary with a sufficient condition. **9.** Confusion of cause and effect. **10.** Neglect of a common cause. **11.** Equivocation. **12.** Is-ought fallacy. **13.** *Post hoc* fallacy. **14.** Syntactical ambiguity. **15.** Causal oversimplification. **16.** Fallacy of composition. **17.** Argument by innuendo. **18.** Domino fallacy. **19.** False alternatives. **20.** Apriorism.

Chapter VI: 1. Assigning irrelevant goals or functions. **2.** Missing the point. **3.** Poisoning the well. **4.** Circumstantial *ad hominem*. **5.** *Tu quoque* argument.

6. Poisoning the well. 7. *Tu quoque* argument. 8. Missing the point. 9. Abusive *ad hominem*. 10. Poisoning the well. 11. *Tu quoque* argument. 12. Loaded or complex question. 13. Fallacy of the continuum. 14. Assigning irrelevant functions or goals. 15. Distinction without a difference. 16. Faulty analogy. 17. Neglect of a common cause. 18. Genetic fallacy. 19. Wishful thinking. 20. Circumstantial *ad hominem*.

Chapter VII: 1. Appeal to tradition. **2.** Appeal to the gallery. **3.** Irrelevant or questionable authority. **4.** Appeal to force or threat. **5.** Appeal to pity. **6.** Appeal to public opinion. **7.** Appeal to pity. **8.** Appeal to the gallery. **9.** Appeal to force or threat. **10.** Appeal to tradition. **11.** Semantical ambiguity. **12.** Is-ought fallacy. **13.** Question-begging definition. **14.** Appeal to public opinion. **15.** Fallacy of novelty. **16.** Fallacy of division. **17.** Causal oversimplification. **18.** Poisoning the well. **19.** Circular reasoning. **20.** Faulty analogy.

Chapter VIII: 1. Red herring. **2.** Resort to humor or ridicule. **3.** Attacking a straw. **4.** Red herring. **5.** Attacking a straw. **6.** Distortion. **7.** Resort to humor or ridicule. **8.** Distortion. **9.** Attacking a straw. **10.** Red herring. **11.** Resort to humor or ridicule. **12.** Missing the point. **13.** Confusion of a necessary with a sufficient condition. **14.** Genetic fallacy. **15.** Argument by innuendo. **16.** Irrelevant or questionable authority. **17.** Appeal to force or threat. **18.** Distortion. **19.** Appeal to tradition. **20.** Misuse of a generalization.

Chapter IX: 1. Insufficient sample. **2.** Fallacy of false precision. **3.** Gambler's fallacy. **4.** Fallacy of false precision. **5.** Insufficient sample. **6.** Gambler's fallacy. **7.** Unrepresentative statistics. **8.** Insufficient sample. **9.** Gambler's fallacy. **10.** Unrepresentative statistics. **11.** Illicit contrast. **12.** Appeal to the gallery. **13.** Assigning irrelevant functions or goals. **14.** Domino fallacy. **15.** Unrepresentative statistics. **16.** Appeal to public opinion. **17.** Irrelevant or questionable authority. **18.** Abusive *ad hominem*. **19.** Circumstantial *ad hominem*. **20.** Confusion of cause and effect.

Chapter X: 1. Illicit distribution of an end term. **2.** Affirming the consequent.[1] **3.** Undistributed middle term. **4.** Illicit distribution of an end term. **5.** False conversion. **6.** Denying the antecedent. **7.** Undistributed middle term. **8.** Denying the antecedent. **9.** Denying the antecedent. **10.** False conversion. **11.** Affirming the consequent. **12.** Inference from a label. **13.** False conversion. **14.** Appeal to pity. **15.** Illicit distribution of an end term. **16.** Affirming the consequent. **17.** Fallacy of the golden mean. **18.** Undistributed middle term. **19.** Fallacy of false precision. **20.** Abusive *ad hominem*.

[1]A number of arguments may be translated into both a syllogistic argument form and a conditional argument form. Hence, the reader may identify some of the fallacies in this chapter differently than I have, depending on how he or she has analyzed the argument.

Index